COOKING IN DOCKLANDS
PAST AND PRESENT

COOKING
IN DOCKLANDS

PAST AND PRESENT

MEAT, FISH AND VEGETABLE RECIPES

Written and illustrated by

JAMES PAGE-ROBERTS

The Mudlark Press

British Library Cataloguing-in-publication data
A catalogue record for this book is available from the British Library

First published in 1998 by The Mudlark Press
PO Box 13729, London W6 9GN

Designed and typeset by Ray Leaning, Smart Credits, 0171 635 7658

Printed and bound by Biddles, Guildford

Cover design by Robert Page-Roberts, 0171 724 9762

ISBN 0 9530517 3 0

CONTENTS

ABOUT THIS BOOK 7

DOCKLAND LIFE 8
THE HOME 8
CHILDREN 10
FOOD IN BAD TIMES 11
FOOD IN BETTER TIMES 13
FISH AND SHELLFISH 14
EELS AND PIES 14
SOME GRUESOME BITS 15
STREET VENDORS 16
RESTAURANT AND CAFE FOOD 17
PUBS AND DRINK 18
HOTELS 19

ABOUT THE RECIPES 20

THE RECIPES 21

A GLOSSARY 123

ITEMS OF ADDITIONAL INTEREST 130
(Children's Games and Sweets,
Cigarettes and Tobacco)

INDEX 131

ABOUT THE AUTHOR 143

I dedicate this book to Margreet, Rob, Pete, Corydon and Brenda Unwin, John Wright, Mrs. Johnson, Brian Thompson, Peggy Gittleson, Ian Hussey, Shirley Shrieber, Maria Gomez, Anthony Murphy, Tom Jacques, Esther O'Sullivan, June MacNaughton, Mr. Conway, Victor and Doreen Harrild, Belle Everett, "Oz" Wheeler, Elio Mizzi, Doug and all the people in shops, old people's homes and pubs for their help, and especially to Amelia (Mill) Phillips who has provided me with so much invaluable first-hand information about inter-war dockland life and cooking.

Books written by the author include:
THE OLDIE COOKBOOK *(Carbery Press)*
GUIDE TO A DOCKLAND OF CHANGE *(Mudlark Press)*
CANARY WHARF AND SIGHTS FROM DOCKLANDS LIGHT RAIL *(Mudlark Press)*
DOCKLAND BUILDINGS OLD AND NEW *(Mudlark Press)*
VINES IN YOUR GARDEN *(Argus Books)*
THE BEST WINE IN THE SUPER MARKET *(Foulsham)*
THE BEST WINE BUYS IN THE HIGH STREET *(Foulsham)* **The first three editions**
VINES AND WINES IN A SMALL GARDEN *(Herbert Press/A&C Black)*
WINES FROM A SMALL GARDEN *(Abeville Press, New York)*
DRUIF EN WIJN UIT EIGEN TUIN *(Schuyt, Haarlem)*
COOKING IN DOCKLANDS PAST AND PRESENT *(Mudlark Press)*

ABOUT THIS BOOK

My main objective in writing this book is to preserve, in a modest way, some details of dockland life and the recipes used by dockers' wives during both good times and bad. I have tried to obtain as much first-hand information about this as possible by talking to people in the area, so that much of my writing on food, drink and domestic circumstances is concerned with the eighty year period starting shortly after the First World War, through to the Second, and beyond. When I refer to food or conditions of earlier times there will be an indication of date or period. I have not included wartime rationing food.

Although it is a fascinating period of history, awareness of its people's lifestyle and food have been much neglected. Fortunately, information lies in the sometimes hazy memory of the more elderly who have lived through some of this time themselves, and are able to recall the way of life and methods of cooking handed down by parents and acquaintances. To the young of today it was a period of deprivation for their parents, and is often purposefully forgotten.

The fare in many East End and dockland homes is still often on the simple, straightforward side, with housewives relying on the recipes of their mothers. However, recent ideas on food, gleaned from newspapers, books, magazines and television, have slowly infiltrated the most modest of kitchens. More imagination is entering the minds of those who once only cooked traditional food. With the availability of ingredients from foreign shores, home cooking has become slightly more exotic.

Vegetarians, incidentally, were either non-existent, very few, or those who, by force of circumstances, could not afford meat. However, I have included many vegetable dishes eaten in dockland homes.

Dockland cooking in the home nowadays can be divided into two parts, or styles. On the one hand there is the kind provided by the wives of hard working dockers of old, the traditionalists, pensioners, and those not well off financially, and on the other, that enjoyed by the people who have become part of an easterly spread of affluent London.

Newcomers to dockland, beside the large Asian influx and those from Council blocks, are often the upwardly mobile who, in the rush to acquire wealth, lack time to prepare and cook food at home. So, rather like the wives of their docker predecessors, who often did not know when their husbands might return from work, simplicity, speed and ease of cooking good food is as important now as it was then.

I have tried, briefly and certainly not comprehensively, to set the scene, then to describe the kind of food eaten in the home and outside it. After that there is information on pubs and drink, before I relate some popular recipes of dockland past and present.

There is also a glossary of many words no longer in use, and lists of games, sweets, cigarette brands and tobacco of the period.

DOCKLAND LIFE

THE HOME

The background for cooking in the depressed inter-war years was a hard one. The typical house for a family of any size had two rooms upstairs, a front room downstairs (if you were posh), and a cosy kitchen/living room. The front room, or parlour, had lino on the floor and was furnished with leather covered chairs and couch, or settee. These were stuffed with horsehair. The better off had a three piece suite covered with leather or rexine, also stuffed with horsehair. The chairs had crocheted antimacassars attached to their backs to prevent hair oil from spoiling them. Crocheted drapes also adorned the mantelpiece. An aspidistra on the polished table or tall stand made a popular house plant for decoration. The front room could also double up as a bedroom with a put-you-up bed, and was used on Sundays. When a member of the household died, the coffin would lie there for a week, when friends and relations could pay their last respects. The blinds would then be closed, as they were in the rest of the street. A candle was kept alight in the room, and lavender oil ensured freshness of the air. A collection was taken for a wreath, with those in the street each contributing a few coppers. Flowers arrived on the day of the funeral. Four black horses, with plumes of feathers on their heads, and over their backs mauve mantles trimmed with gold and gold tassels, drew the hearse and carriages for the mourners.

Outside at the back of the house was a small yard with space for drying laundry on lines, a water tap, lean-to lavatory usually containing torn-up newspaper threaded on to a loop of string (a job for the children), washhouse, or scullery, with wooden-lidded copper, and a mangle. A zinc, human-sized bath (called a bungalow bath) would be hanging on the wall, with sometimes a smaller, oval one, or half a barrel for clothes washing. Those who used a barrel might well use the other half for rinsing.

White washing was put into the copper with water and Hudson's or Carbosil soap powder and boiled until clean and sparkling white. Then in would go the rest of the washing. The water in this copper was heated from within a whitewashed brick and stone container below the bowl, using cardboard or wood gathered by the children. The copper also supplied boiling water for the zinc bath - an essential for dockers and stevedores after handling filthy or obnoxious cargo. When one lady used the copper to boil her Christmas pudding for 12 hours, the bed linen and towels smelt of mixed spice for quite a time afterwards. Life was easier when gas coppers were introduced in the 1930s. Public baths were also used, when they were handy. Housewives might do their laundry at the public wash house, where they would take their own soap and washing powder.

Clothes were scrubbed on a washboard and put through the mangle (or wringer) to squeeze out most of the moisture. Fingers might get caught, and if the rollers were set too close together, buttons would break. The mangle was also used to press laundry to give it an ironed look when dry folded. Blue was used, in the form of a blue bag, and the washing starched before ironing. The centre of dockland life was the kitchen. It was a warm haven for both adult and child, smelling of cooking, washing, carbolic soap, cigarette and pipe smoke. Its life and food form the heart of this book.

The centerpiece of the kitchen was the black, open fire range with its hob, trivets and oven. Fuel for it was coal or coke. Cooking ranges were often beautiful objects and ones in which the housewife took great pride, along with (whiting) the front doorstep and (blackleading) the door knocker. The ironwork was shiny with blacking, and the firebox glowed with red hot coals. The ranges sometimes incorporated swivel trivets that swung out for hot irons. And below the fire a grid came out for the kettle and stew pots. Trivets could also be hooked to the bars of the firebox, and such as herring or Yarmouth bloaters hung from the upper one to grill in front of the coals. A container on another trivet or grid below would catch the drips. For ironing clothes, these trivets were used to keep two irons hot. When one became cool, the other would be ready (having been spat upon to test for adequate temperature). The hot and heavy flat irons were taken off the trivets in a cloth holder. Most claim that these old-fashioned irons made a far better job than the electric ones of today.

Coal smoke from so many ranges created an acrid smell in the air and contributed to the many thick fogs of the past. Chimneys had to be swept regularly, as soot could clog the dampers and flues. The flues were swept with great care and the soot collected at the lowest soot door. Blacklead, to enhance the beauty of these objects of pride, was moistened with water, or turpentine to gain the shiniest results. To save the cost of employing a chimney sweep, many people with open fires would set the chimney alight, with the resultant roar of noise, foul smell and dense, air polluting smoke. Coal was sometimes delivered in 1 cwt. or ½ cwt. bags to the coal bunker in the yard, or tipped into a cupboard beneath the stairs from the passage leading from the street door. For those living upstairs the coal would be tipped into a cupboard under the dresser.

A large cast iron kettle on the trivet or hob of the range would keep water hot for tea, cocoa, coffee and washing up. Greasy items were cleaned with hot water and washing soda. The range's oven was a place not only for baking pies and tarts, etc., but also to heat bricks that were then wrapped in cloth to warm the bed in wintertime.

In front of the range often stood a rack with wet clothes to dry or laundry to air. And for those who took in washing, it could be hanging on lines in the kitchen and in the passage.

Gas lighting was introduced into many homes around the turn of the century using jets and mantles. Some houses had gas rings. Gas stoves began to replace kitchen ranges in the 1930s. There were then explosions, and because coal gas was poisonous, easier suicides. Gas supply came through a penny slot meter (a shilling in the 1950s) placed high up on a wall. The meters were emptied by the gas man who counted the pennies, left a refund, returned a few coppers to the box, and took away the rest in a bag.

Some houses did not have electricity until the 1930s. Initially, supply was only DC current.

Kitchen tables were scoured with bar soap and a scrubbing brush - always rubbed along the grain of the wood. Lime and sand were sometimes used instead of soap. The table doubled up as an ironing board, when it was covered first with a blanket and then a piece of sheet on top of that. Boots and shoes were often mended in the home. Working boots were treated with dubbin to waterproof them and preserve the leather.

It was common practice to visit the pawnbroker on Monday and redeem goods on Friday after receiving the pay packet. On items pawned for 5/-, 5/3d would be demanded at the end of the week. After 3 months the pawnbroker was free to sell the goods. And when neighbours fell on hard times or there were sick to be looked after, there was such a sense of mutual support that help and food were nearly always at hand. This was in the days when no-one bothered to lock their doors. Doors are now well locked, if not double locked and more. That past sense of community now exists mainly among family and friends.

Even in the dreadful depression years of the early 1930s, people recall the pleasures more than the hardships of not having enough money for food and clothing.

CHILDREN

No-one can remember being bored as children. Games were invented, and home-made balls booted around. There was scrounging for anything to sell, and ruses to make money for sweets, like cutting through sacks of corn on the delivery cart, then to bag up the grain to sell in small quantities as chicken feed. There were endless and imaginative games and ways of keeping happy and busy (see page 130 for some games).

When children had earned money by legal or illegal means, or been given some for sweets, they might buy four items for a penny - a farthing each. Posh kids bought 1 oz. for a penny. The poorer managed to obtain 2 oz. a penny. Or for a halfpenny the poorer ones might get the full penny's worth. The choice was enormous (see page 130 for some sweets). And if anyone nicked some Exlax chocolate by mistake, the laxative would soon take effect and surprise the thief. And Andrew's Liver Salt fizzed and did look rather like sherbet.

Cigarette cards were added to packets of cigarettes (and tea), with children collecting, swapping and glueing them into albums supplied by the makers. The subjects of these cards were many and various, with cricketers, footballers, the military, butterflies, birds, flowers and railway engines among them. Also from cigarette packets came miniature playing cards that could be swapped for a real pack when complete.

The ice-cream man came around to sell his delicious custard ices from a lidded round tin within another tin filled with ice. It cost ½d a tiny cornet. The children's cry was "Okey pokey, penny a lump, the more you eat, the more you jump".

FOOD IN BAD TIMES

A woman's lot in the days of working docks was not easy. It was they who often worked for a second wage, ran the house, cared for children - and cooked. With their menfolk's ability to obtain dock work often a lottery, life for families connected with that industry could be very hard indeed.

Ingredients for the kitchen had to be cheap, the dishes simple. Food for dockers, lightermen and stevedores, because of the vagaries of time, tide and movement of labour, had often to be quick to prepare. Long and slow cooking was also usual, with food sometimes to be kept hot over a period of time. The kitchen range, being alight for most of the time, encouraged slow cooking.

But the primary considerations of those who cooked in harder and less prosperous days were cheap cuts of meat and economical ingredients with stomach-filling properties. Certain dishes fell directly into these categories. Steamed puddings, made with both meat and sweet ingredients, were very popular for their belly-filling and strength-giving properties. The suet crust pastry needed for them was easy to make, and cheap. The extra cost of fuel to keep the puddings steaming for hours was not always a consideration, as the kitchen range was the constant source of heat for the house in wintertime.

With money in short supply, the children might be sent to the corner shop for a pennyworth of salmon and shrimp paste, mustard pickles or jam. These would be sold loose and uncovered from stoneware jars or basins. The customer would bring a cup, which was first weighed empty, and then after a pennyworth of this or that had been ladled into it with a long handled spoon, weighed again. Sugar was sold in a "blue poke" in 1/2 lbs.

For breakfast the children might be given hot porridge oats, taking two slices of toast, wrapped in newspaper, to school, which started at 9 a.m. Dinner time was 12.30 p.m. They would come home at 4 p.m. for tea of bread and jam, syrup or dripping, or possibly bread pudding. Some children would not be given breakfast, but on their way to school would collect 1½d worth of hot bread pudding from the baker.

A stockpot was to be found in some kitchens into which went every scrap of bone, gristle or trimming to make stock for soups and gravy.

Hunks of bread and jam were popular in the home and at theatrical entertainments. Treacle (golden syrup) was much used on bread and in puddings. Bread and dripping was, by tradition, a staple. If there was money for a beef roast, it would have been coated with a layer of fat and possibly have extra fat added. The melted "drippings" from this cooking were poured into a dripping pot or basin and allowed to cool and harden. The dripping was used for cooking and spread on bread or toast, sprinkled with salt (obtained from a block), and eaten with great pleasure. Bread and dripping was always a poor man's food, and a "perk" for the staff of larger establishments. The employers were either not allowed it or declined to eat such a lowly food to which their staff had a "right". The toffs were missing a considerable delicacy - especially when some jelly from the bottom of the dripping pot was added by being stirred into the rest.

It was not the custom to bake one's own bread, though the Irish made soda bread.

Sausages and mash with fried onions was a very popular dish. Dumplings were a dockland favourite. They were added to soups and stews to make them go further and fill the stomach and, being easy to prepare, with only chopped fat, flour and salt as the ingredients, were cheap, satisfying and filling. They were sometimes eaten with salt beef and carrots (a tremendous favourite), the salted meat being preserved in brine in the days before refrigeration (see the Glossary for details). Yorkshire pudding, known as batter pudding, and black jack, also fell into this "simple and cheap to make" category, as did jam dumplings and that dockland favourite, bread pudding. Soup was always warming, nourishing, cheap to make and filling. Edward's Soup Granules, at 2p a packet, were used. But the favourite, was split pea, cooked with bacon bones. Bacon bones were also used to flavour stews. Other soups eaten were lentil, potato, and leek and potato.

Available herbs were parsley, sage (for sage and onion stuffing with poultry) and thyme (for stews). But herbs were not used a great deal. The spices in use were mainly pepper, cloves (for apple tarts), mace (for soups and stews), nutmeg (for rice, junket and tapioca pudding), bay leaf (for pickling), allspice (for bread puddings, cakes and pickling), mixed spice (for bread pudding), caraway seeds (for cakes), cinnamon (for bread pudding, cakes and stewed fruits) and dill in Jewish households.

The fruit available were oranges, lemons, apples and pears, with cherries, strawberries and other soft fruit in season. Vegetables for sale were pot herbs (see Glossary), potatoes, cauliflower, onions, carrots, leeks, lettuce, cabbage (very popular), Brussels sprouts, parsnips, swede and turnips. Garlic was virtually unheard of, with demand so small that even the Breton onion seller did not offer it. Mushrooms do not seem to have featured until after WW2. Lettuce salads were often a Sunday treat, with home-made coleslaw also a favourite.

Rice was eaten as rice pudding and sometimes in soups and stews, especially when pearl barley was unavailable. Pearl barley was put into many a soup and stew, and was most popular. Dried beans were used as a vegetable when soaked overnight and boiled. Haricot and butter beans were popular. Lentils were also used in stews and soups, and dried split peas were by far the most used as the main ingredient for pease pudding and pea and bacon bone soup.

FOOD IN BETTER TIMES

Although times were often hard, the thrifty and imaginative wife of a docker or casual labourer could do surprisingly well in the way of meals. A typical menu for the week could be a roast of beef (with strong horseradish sauce) or lamb with batter pudding and mixed vegetables on Sunday. On Monday there would be cold meat from the larder (kept on the north side of the house, – and no-one can recall food poisoning) with mashed potato and mustard pickles or brown sauce, the two latter being bought loose and in bottle. These might be followed by tinned fruit and custard. On Tuesday, Wednesday and Thursday there could be meat pie, meat pudding (steamed), stews of beef, lamb, rabbit or sausage, liver and bacon, ox-tail, salt beef (home pickled as it was sometimes thought to be too expensive when obtained from the butcher) and pease pudding. Also favoured were stuffed hearts cooked in the oven, corned beef pie and toad-in-the-hole or shepherd's pie. Afters might be sago, semolina, blancmange, tapioca, junket, jelly or rice pudding.

In some houses there would be no cooking on Fridays, so fish and chips, faggots and pease pudding or saveloys with pease pudding were popular. And the children might get half a kipper for tea. On Saturdays sausages and mash with fried onions and gravy were often on the menu, and split pea soup would be kept hot on the hob all day.

The docker might not return until 6 o'clock for his dinner. Then those in the family at work would enjoy their hot meal together, having eaten sandwiches for the 12.30 p.m. break. Food might be stew, steamed pudding, smoked haddock, kippers or bloaters. A late supper at 10 o'clock for the man of the house could be pig's trotters (very popular) or bread, raw Spanish onion and cheese, pared off against the thumb with a penknife.

Sunday dinner of a roast would not be eaten until 2 o'clock as the man of the house would not return from the pub until it closed at that time. It was he who carved the joint, presumably sometimes unsteadily of foot and hand.

Sunday teas at 6.30 p.m. were a great and "posh" treat. A tablecloth was laid over the scrubbed pine table and spread with winkles, shrimps, watercress and celery. There would also be fruitcake and real butter for the bread, – instead of every-day margarine.

In good times the housewife might buy an aitchbone of beef. This hip section of the animal would supply a large family with a roast, and meat for stews and mince for a week. It was primarily a roasting joint, and popular at Christmas time.

Meat was also boiled or stewed in iron pots, as was cabbage. In the oven could be meat and potatoes, though when there was meat to roast on Sunday, it was often taken to the baker for him to cook in his bread oven. He charged according to the size of the pan. Jewish bakers would cook pots of cholent overnight. These pots of meat and vegetables would anyhow be too large for the domestic oven. Bagels were not made in the home but always available from the bakers.

Pancakes were eaten, but almost exclusively on Shrove Tuesday, pancake day. Pasta has been a comparatively recent introduction, with the exception of macaroni, and vermicelli, used in stews and Jewish chicken soup.

FISH AND SHELLFISH

A favourite fish to eat in the home was herring. As a boy in the 1920s, I remember being taught at school that herrings were among the most plentiful, nutritious and cheapest of foods. And I am sure they were. Other popular derivations of the herring were kippers, Yarmouth bloaters, red herrings and rollmops. Also eaten in dockland were eels, conger eel, plaice, dabs, haddock, cod, sprats, whitebait and Arbroath smokies.

Outside pubs (with a site on the main road when possible) at weekends were often to be seen, and still are sometimes, shellfish stalls, known as shrimp and winkle stalls. These covered stalls provided customers with bowls or plates containing one or a mix of any of the seafood offered, to eat there or take away. The choice was, and is, shrimps (pink and brown), prawns, whelks, winkles, cockles, rollmops, jellied eels, crabs, oysters and mussels. The jellied eels often came from a chipped, enamelled basin. And they still can. On a shelf in front of the stall were small dishes of cockles at 6d a go. Customers would add vinegar and stand around eating.

The winkle men also toured the streets on Sundays with the same offerings but with watercress and scrubbed celery added. The shellfish was bought for tea. Shrimp and winkle stalls, with their attendants, once a great tradition of East End life, are seen less and less.

EELS AND PIES

Since Georgian days, the real East End food speciality has been eel pies, and later, when food shops opened in Victorian and Edwardian days, pie and mash and sometimes eels.

Eel pies have gone out of favour with the increasing cost of eels. And although jellied eels are sometimes available, stewed eels are often on the eel and pie shop's daily or week-end menu, to be eaten with mash and parsley sauce (liquor), or combined with meat pies, mash and parsley sauce.

Parsley sauce covers these dishes, just as custard covers steamed puddings and fruit pies, etc. The busy and successful pie and mash shop owner makes the two sauces in great quantity, often offering the customer extra parsley sauce on the pies and mash ordered. Many customers add vinegar, of the non-brewed condiment variety.

Mash varies considerably. It usually lacks salt, which seems very strange when the taste of mashed potato is so much better when adequate salt has been combined at the mashing stage. But salt is always on offer at the tables, sometimes in huge shakers.

The pie pastry also varies from being fairly light to quite heavy. The quality of meat used also varies according to its cook. Minced beef inside the pies may be on the dry side or combined with plenty of gravy. With the gravied kind your plate can be awash with a gravy/parsley liquid. The filling in the pies surprisingly lacks onion, and is not as a rule more than lightly seasoned.

Eels are cut into small pieces and stewed in liquor. Tepid, they are taken out of the pot with a perforated spoon and counted carefully before being put on a plate or in a bowl. If they have been in the liquid for some time, the pieces lose firmness and flavour. Tail pieces are added and, if ordered especially, may come as a more generous helping. The bone is always in, and has to be extracted in the mouth with the help of teeth and an agile tongue. However contrived, the result is generally delicious.

Eel and pie shops are almost invariably spartan in aspect and comfort, featuring narrow and hard bench seats, sometimes marble topped tables, perhaps sawdust on the floor, and often with patterned tiles on wall surfaces. When I lived in dockland in the 1960s, I would make my way to Bow from Limehouse to eat in an eel and pie shop there. And because the spoons provided were not of the most inviting kind, I took my own. This practice is no longer necessary.

Fruit pies or steamed puddings and custard are sometimes offered to follow the eels, pies and mash. But after eels or pie and mash, double pie and double mash, possibly with eels as well, there is seldom room in the belly for more. Hard labour engenders a healthy appetite, and it is not an uncommon sight to see enormous quantities of food consumed in an eel and pie shop by market men, lorry drivers or building site workers.

But whichever food is eaten in these eel and pie shops, and in whatever quantity, the price of it is almost invariably reasonable. Good value and a good helping is part of the eel and pie shop's heritage, and is still their present policy. Long may these dockland institutions survive as unique marks on the food landscape of the East End.

SOME GRUESOME BITS
(to be skipped by the faint-hearted)

There was no time for squeamishness in the dockland days of old. Chickens lived in many a back yard, fed mainly on scraps and boiled potato peelings mixed with bran. Their eggs were preserved in earthenware jars of isinglass or waterglass for when the chickens were in moult and unproductive. The birds were slaughtered by stretching their necks and plucking and trussing them for Christmas or at the end of their egg-laying days. Then they tended to find their way into either the roasting tin, or the boiling pot to be coated with parsley sauce. The water in which they were boiled became soup or replenishment liquid for the stockpot.

Cows were kept in yards for their milk and their bull calves sold or slaughtered for meat. A cow beyond its usefulness became meat for pies, offal (tripe and brains were popular and cheap), feet, hide, jelly and glue. Nothing was wasted.

Pigs, too, were housed in many a back yard for their meat. And when killed (without much finesse and with a lot of noise), nothing was wasted from the carcass. Ears, tail, chaps, brain, tongue, heart, liver, lights, kidneys, muscle meat, head meat for sausages and brawn, fat, skin and trotters were all prized and relished. At the killing, the blood was drained into a bowl to be mixed with grain and pieces of fat. This mixture was forced into the pig's cleaned entrails to become black pudding. When the bones had had all the goodness boiled out of them for stock or soup, they were given to a dog. All was utilised, except, I think, the teeth and eyes. Perhaps there was a use for them as well.

Sheep went much the same way, feet and all, with nothing wasted from the fleece inwards.

Eels, that much loved delicacy of the region, were bought alive from the fishmonger or stall and, after decapitation and gutting at a stroke, the still wriggling and lashing-out eel would be put into a bag to be taken home and cut into small pieces.

For those who would catch their own, eels were caught in traps, on hook and line, with specially designed, trident-shaped spears and in a most unpleasant way involving a dead dog.

In earlier times, snails were marketed as walfish or dew slugs and fed for a week on a diet of bran, porridge, lettuce, onion and water. Then, after being simmered for 20 minutes, they were extracted from their shells and stewed in a strong mixture of herbs and spices or put into pies. Some soaked the snails for 2 hours in salt and vinegar before boiling them.

People growing up in the hamburger age sometimes even decline to eat a dish in which there are bones. One dockland lady was put off eating anything on the bone when, as a child, a family treat was a sheep's head brought to the table on a huge dish surrounded by vegetables.

STREET VENDORS

From the 18th century and earlier to before WW2, many foods were sold by street vendors from their wagons, carts, barrows or from baskets on their heads. The salesmen and women shouted out their wares, each in a very distinctive way. They and their cries were recorded in a series of prints entitled "The Cries of London". Several artists contributed to this series toward the end of the 18th and early 19th centuries. "Scarlet Strawberries", "New Mackerel" and "Hot Spice Gingerbread Smoking Hot" were among them. The fishmonger would call out that he was selling Dutch herrings, haddocks, conger eel, dabs, plaice, sprats, mussels and whelks. The muffin man rang a hand bell and carried his muffins in a tray on his head (one came to our remote village in the country in the 1930s). There were cries from those selling celery and watercress, wild rabbits, skimmed milk, salt and vinegar, calf's foot and pig's trotters, salt beef and hot pies. Among the last street cries to be heard were those of the rag and bone man, shrimp and winkle man ("shrimps and winkles all fresh today"), the cats' meat man, the knife and scissor sharpener, salt man ("don't forget your salt, Ma, penny a lump"), Breton onion sellers, the Indian toffee man and those selling ice-cream from their pedal tricycle carts (Stop Me And Buy One). A lady told me that she could recall a Jewish seller of fruit, who also shouted out his wares. He was the only Jew allowed "across the bridge" into Wapping.

RESTAURANT AND CAFE FOOD

Early eating places took the form of coffee stalls. These became very common when the duty on coffee was reduced in 1842. Open night and day, they were situated near to horse troughs for their water supply, obtained from a tap at one end. They served tea as well as coffee and cocoa. A range of sandwiches was on offer, with bacon, sausage, ham, dripping, corned beef, fish paste, brawn, egg, and eggs and bacon among them. Should a client not feel well, or suffer from a hangover or in need of a laxative, instant cures were always available for sale at these stalls in the form of Beecham's Pills ("Worth a Guinea a Box"), Seidlitz powders, Rochelle, Bile Beans and Movies, if not Syrup of Figs.

Daytime cafes continue to abound in dockland, and offer enormous breakfasts of bacon, eggs, fried slice, beans, tomatoes, chips, sausages, mushrooms, toast and tea. This combination is offered throughout the day. At mid-day the menu consists of stews, meat, steak and kidney pies and puddings, with boiled, mash, bubble, peas, chips and gravy. This is followed by such as steamed jam or treacle roll, plain and syrup, stewed apple, college pudding or spotted dog. Puddings are served with custard. Tea is the drink, with instant coffee offered since that was introduced. Buns and cake to have with tea are presented from behind glass display cabinets. Building and office workers frequent them. Smarter editions and coffee bars are now housed within the Canary Wharf complex.

Few families ate out in the days of the working docks, and there was an almost total lack of restaurants in the East End of London. The exceptions were the fish and chip shops, which many found to be too expensive and thus a great treat to visit, the Chinese restaurants around Limehouse, the eel, pie and mash shops so loved by the locals (to this day) and cafes and dining rooms providing substantial fried and steamed fare for those needing warmth and energy in the course of a day's work.

The Chinese restaurants that attracted local and "up west" customers to Limehouse are fewer but still there. Chinese takeaways are now established in other parts of dockland. Eel and pie shops remain, but although new ones do appear, the traditional, old-fashioned dockland establishments are losing ground. Thai and Indian restaurants, with their takeaways, have blossomed recently throughout the East End and become very popular. Smart restaurants come and go in their attempt to lure the affluent newcomers who live or work in the area. Burger chains continue to burgeon and pizza places proliferate.

PUBS AND DRINK

Dockers, through the need to replenish lost moisture and the desire for entertainment, of which there was often little available, frequented the plethora of that most British of institutions, the pub. Many of these establishments were warm and cosy, resplendent with dark mahogany fittings, cut glass panels, yellow-smoked paintwork on embossed ceilings, and frosted, cut glass windows so that the inquisitive could not see in from the outside. Men would sometimes spend more of their wages than they should on beer. This, in turn, led to drunkenness and sometimes violence in the home. And that, in turn, led to procreation and more mouths to feed. Children needed clothing as well as their parents, and that meant less money for food.

With an off-licence section in the pub, and customers to serve in the Lounge bar (the most expensive and where you might take your grandmother), Saloon bar (middle price range where you would take wives or girl friends – no swearing) and Public bar (the cheapest, roughest and where there was a darts board) and possibly Snug bar, publicans seldom had the time or staff to offer food, except for possibly arrowroot biscuits. These rock-hard biscuits were bought for the children who waited outside when their parents were drinking within. Recently, publicans have discovered that there is good profit to be made by providing menus, both simple and elaborate, of indigenous and foreign fare.

Fads in the taste for beer constantly change – stout, porter, mild, brown ale, bitter, light and bitter, ginger beer shandy, real ale, ice this and that, lager, lager and lime... and on it will go – and change again. Boys tended to start on brown ale.

Although beer is still the most popular drink in dockland for both sexes, women were once very fond of port and lemon (a measure of ruby port and a bottle of lemonade) and Milk Stout. Gin has been popular since being introduced in the early 18th century by soldiers returning from wars through Holland. Shrub was once served. Vodka is now the most popular spirit, followed by whisky and gin.

For all classes, wine has made considerable inroads, with those new to the drink starting with sweeter varieties and changing to drier as their tastes develop. Fortified wines, like port and sherry, have declined in popularity, mainly, I think, because of their sometimes high cost, and also high alcohol content (20% and 15%-17% respectively).

The methylated spirit and brown boot polish brigade have upgraded to cans of strong lager or large plastic bottles of cider. Pubs selling only cider, cider houses, have disappeared. They, their clientele and smell are not missed.

Smoking was commonplace in pubs, at work and in the home (for a list of cigarette brands and tobacco see page 130). No-one had connected the use of tobacco with cancer or other diseases.

HOTELS

There were very few hotels in the East End, simply because no outsiders needed to visit or stay in the district. Businessmen came into the dockland area by the day to organise commerce and negotiate with powerful Unions for the required labour. Now hotels spring up almost by the day to cater for business visitors from home and overseas.

ABOUT THE RECIPES

As in dockland cooking past and present, the theme of the following recipes is simplicity. All recipes, from both past and present, are easy to prepare. The ingredients are readily available. Time taken in preparing the dishes is minimal. Cooking times are usually short, though one or two dishes do need long cooking at a low heat, as in the case of some dockland recipes of old, when the stove was alight all day.

Because it is not possible to separate old and new recipes, they will be jumbled together to, I hope, delight the reader.

I cannot claim to have prepared every dish mentioned in this book. Faggots, for instance, involving grinding up windpipes, lungs and spleen, etc., is, I believe, best left to the butcher. Sheep's head is not available at present, and I am not going to waste 10 or more hours in preparing and cooking tripe, which I do not like anyway.

No account has been taken of food "scares", which come and go.

My cooking times, weights and measures are cursory. The kind of cooking facilities in your kitchen, with your own experience of them and judgement, should be enough, though I do offer indications. So it has been a most pleasant surprise to learn that this approach is, and was, very common in dockland.

The cost of cooking the dishes in this book will be far less than 'instant', pre-prepared and microwaved fare, and obtained at a mere fraction of the money demanded when eating out.

The recipes are penned in such a clear and simple way that children wanting to take part in the household cooking will feel at home with them.

Simplicity and good food, just as it always has been in the dock area of London's East End, is what this book is all about. I do hope you enjoy it.

Any weights and measures mentioned will be pre-metrication, as it was then. However, quick conversion where wanted is approximately as follows:

LIQUID:	SOLID:
1/4 pt. = 140ml.,	1/2 oz. = 14g.,
1/2 pt. = 275ml.,	1oz. = 28g.,
1 pint = 570ml.	2oz. = 56g.,
	1/4 lb. = 112g.,
	1/2 lb. = 225g.,
	1lb. = 450g.,
	2lb. 3oz. = 1kg.

THE RECIPES

FIRST COURSES

BOILED SUET PUDDING AND GRAVY 25
TOMATO SALAD 26
THREE COLOURED SALAD 27
GRATED CARROT SALAD 27
CARROTS WITH GARLIC, BUTTER AND PARSLEY 28
MUSHROOMS 29
AVOCADOS AND FILLINGS 30
HUMMUS 31
RED BEANS AND HOT DRESSING 32
RICE SALAD 33
OMELETTES 34

VEGETABLES ALONE

PEASE PUDDING 35
PLAIN AND DELICIOUS MASHED POTATO 36
MASH VARIATIONS 37
POTATO PANCAKES 38
POTATOES AND ONIONS BAKED IN MILK 39
BUBBLE AND SQUEAK 39
FRIED POTATOES AND ONIONS, AND SPANISH OMELETTE 40
ROAST POTATOES 41
CAULIFLOWER CHEESE 42
CAULIFLOWER WITH GARLIC AND FRIED BREADCRUMBS 43
BRUSSELS SPROUTS BOILED WITH BUTTER, THEN FRIED 44
CLASSIC GRILLED TOMATOES 45
FRIED PEPPERS, AND MORE 46

SAUCES

Custards and Bread and Butter Pudding 47
Parsley Sauce 49
White Sauce 49
White Sauces for Vegetables - and much else 50
Basic Meat Sauce 51
Mayonnaise 53
Vinaigrette 54
Chinese Curry Sauce 55
Some Sauces for Pasta 56
Cold and Hot Dip Sauces 57
Gravy and Oxo Gravy 58
Sharp Gravy 59
Mint Sauce and Mint Gravy 60
Horseradish Sauce 60
Bread Sauce 61
Ice-cream Sauces 62
Hot Chocolate Sauce for Ice-cream 63

SOUPS

Leek and Potato Soup 64
Stock 65
Pea and Bacon Bone Soup 66
Cream of Tuna Fish Soup 67
Other Cream Soups 68
Chicken Soup 68
Artichoke Soup 69
Pumpkin Soup 70
Watercress Soup 71
Dumplings for Soup (and stews) 72

PASTA

Spaghetti with Meat Sauce 73
Pop's Pasta 75
Macaroni Cheese 77

MAIN COURSES

VEGETABLES, FISH AND MEAT

Meat Pudding (and Jam Dumplings) 78
Medieval Beef Stew 79
Egg and Tomato Pie 80
Fish Cakes 81
Eels and Eel Pie 82
Corned Beef Hash and Corned Beef Pie 83
Irish Stew 84
Boiled Salt Beef or Pork 85
Tuna Fish Pie 86
Tuna and Beans 87
Chilli con Carne 88
Cottage and Shepherd's Pie with a Vegetarian Alternative 89
Lamb Stew, Beef Stew, Sausage Stew, Rabbit Stew,
and Sausage and Smoked Bacon Stew 90
Curried Mince and Peas 91
Pig's Trotters 92
Pig's Head 93
Sheep's Head and Calf's Head 94
Calf's Foot and Cow Heel 95
Cabbage, Potatoes, Sausage, etc. 96
Liver and Bacon 97
Thick Cheese Pancake 98
Faggots and Faggot Stew 99
Yorkshire Pudding (Batter Pudding) and Black Jack 100
Toad-in-the-Hole 101
Ox-Tail 101
Tripe and Onions 102

SWEETS

HEDGEHOG COFFEE CAKE 103
FLAPJACKS 104
ICE-CREAM OF VARIOUS KINDS 105
BREAD PUDDING 106
THIN PANCAKES 107
LARGE FRUIT CAKE, SEED(Y) CAKE, COCONUT CAKE 109
SHORT CRUST PASTRY 110
SUET CRUST PASTRY 111
APPLE TART, MINCE TART, JAM TART AND TURNOVERS 112
RUSTIC APPLE PIE 113
STEAMED PUDDINGS – STEAK AND KIDNEY, SAUSAGE AND ONION, VEGETABLE,
TREACLE PUDDING, SPOTTED DOG, SPOTTED DICK, AND JAM ROLY-POLY.
(*See also* MEAT PUDDING on page 78 FOR JAM DUMPLINGS.) 114
JUNKET 115
RICE PUDDING, TAPIOCA PUDDING, SEMOLINA AND SAGO 116
BLANCMANGE 117

ODDS AND ENDS

THAT DO NOT FIT IN ELSEWHERE

DRIPPING 118
MARINATED OLIVES 119
PORRIDGE 119
MAKING BREAD 120
CHEESE STRAWS 121
MAKING CHILLI CON CARNE POWDER 122

FIRST COURSES

Although we start, quite naturally, with first courses, they were almost unheard of in the dockland of old. The first course was the main course, followed by a sweet pudding of some sort. So, keeping to the dockland theme of simplicity and economy, the first course section will consist mostly of modern recipes.

Suet puddings in many forms were favourites in dockland. Simple to make, with cheap ingredients, and a cooking range alight for most of the time on which to steam them, suet puddings were often available in the home.

To prepare the stomach for the main food to come, some dockers would eat a slice of hot, cold or fried suet pudding and gravy. That is the nearest I can find to a first course.

So let us plunge into the deep and stodgy end with a dockland recipe which would find little favour today:

BOILED SUET PUDDING AND GRAVY

For this you will need:
Steamed suet pudding
Gravy

To make the pudding
see Suet Crust Pastry on page 111,
Steamed Puddings on page 114,
and the recipe for Gravy and Oxo Gravy on page 58.

The instructions would be simply to put them together and tuck in.

***

Starting as we will continue, with dishes of simplicity, speed and economy, this first course of more modern times is one that will whet the appetite rather than stifle it. The main ingredient is tomato, not those from cans that almost invariably accompany a breakfast in a dockland cafe, but fresh ones, slightly unripe and firm. The dish is a classic of simplicity, and may be prepared well before the meal, allowing time for other things. It is welcoming to both eye and stomach.

TOMATO SALAD

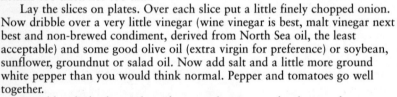

For the salad you will need:
Tomatoes, preferably slightly under ripe
Onion
Oil
Vinegar
Pepper and salt
Parsley or sweet basil

Cut out the cores of tomatoes (where they were attached to their stems). Do not bother to peel them. Cut the tomatoes to make slices that are neither too thick nor too thin.

Lay the slices on plates. Over each slice put a little finely chopped onion. Now dribble over a very little vinegar (wine vinegar is best, malt vinegar next best and non-brewed condiment, derived from North Sea oil, the least acceptable) and some good olive oil (extra virgin for preference) or soybean, sunflower, groundnut or salad oil. Now add salt and a little more ground white pepper than you would think normal. Pepper and tomatoes go well together.

Sprinkle a little chopped parsley over the top or a few leaves of sweet basil torn up in the fingers. That's it.

Be sure to serve the tomatoes with some crusty bread to dip into the lovely juices.

* * *

The following would never have appeared on the tables of old dockland, as avocados are a comparatively recent introduction to the greengrocer's display. Of Italian origins, it is very much a first course of modern docklands. It is really a variation of tomato salad, but being a little more elaborate and looking rather nicer on the plates at table, it is more of a party salad. Anyhow, it is easy to prepare and can be done a little time before your friends arrive.

THREE COLOURED SALAD

For this you will need:
Tomatoes
Avocado pears
Mozzarella cheese or feta cheese
Vinaigrette dressing (see page 54)

Slice tomatoes and lay a few on each
plate. Peel an avocado pear by first
slicing it in half in the direction of
round to point and giving the halves
a twist in opposite directions. Extract the pip with the point of a knife and
peel off the green skin. Slice the yellow flesh lengthwise and arrange the
pieces next to the tomato on the plate. Now cut up either mozzarella or feta
cheese and put this between the tomato and avocado. Now pour some
vinaigrette (page 54) over all. Decorate with a few torn basil leaves. Serve
with some crusty bread with which to mop up the juices on the plate.

***

Carrots in dockland were either plain boiled on the hob or added to stews.
This is a simple first course or vegetarian dish. Only taking a little time to
grate the carrots and squeeze a lemon, it nearly breaks my record for speed
and simplicity. So it pleases me
doubly on the account of time
taken to prepare it and for its
excellent and clean taste.
Accordingly, the instructions for
making it are minimal, too.

GRATED CARROT SALAD

For this you will need:
Carrots
Oil of your choice
Lemon

Clean the carrots, being very careful to discard quite a bit of the top where
the poisonous chemicals for combating carrot root fly might lie. Grate the
carrots and to them add oil and lemon juice to taste.

***

This is another way to turn the humble carrot into a dish with style. It is simple and straightforward to make, and will please meat-eaters and vegetarians alike. It is very economical, too. Use it as a first course alone, as a main course for vegetarians, or as a vegetable to accompany meat or fish.

CARROTS WITH GARLIC, BUTTER AND PARSLEY

For this you will need:
Carrots
Garlic
Butter
Pepper and salt
Parsley

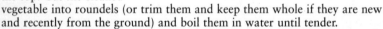

Clean carrots well by scraping off the outer skin layer with the edge of a sharp knife and trimming off either end - cutting more from the top. Cut the cleaned vegetable into roundels (or trim them and keep them whole if they are new and recently from the ground) and boil them in water until tender.

Strain them (retaining the water possibly to start or dilute a soup) and return the saucepan to the stove to evaporate any residual moisture.

Now add a good lump of butter, pepper and salt, a clove of garlic squeezed in a garlic press and chopped parsley. Turn it all around over low heat until the carrot pieces are quite coated with butter, garlic and parsley, and serve.

This excellent method of cooking a vegetable may be used successfully with other than carrots. The principle is the same. Try French beans, runner beans or broad beans. Pulses, too, when soaked and cooked, respond well to the treatment. Try another fresh herb, like coriander.

* * *

Mushrooms do not seem to have featured on dockland menus until after WW2. If they did they were the field variety and seasonal or dried. Now they, and many another edible fungi, are available in many shapes and sizes. They can be served on their own, mixed with vegetables or meats as a first or main course, fried, grilled, served raw, marinated, vinaigretted, sauced, souped, casseroled... They are versatile to say the least.

Let us concentrate here on a way of serving a few as a first course or more as a main course for vegetarians. Incidentally, garlic goes well with mushrooms, but of course it is not necessary, and was seldom ever used in dockland of old. Here is the first suggestion:

MUSHROOMS

For this you will need:
Oil
Vinegar
Garlic (optional)
Mushrooms
Pepper and salt
Parsley

Heat a generous amount of oil and vinegar in a frying pan until you can sniff the steam without discomfort. The steaming vinegar will be very strong at first and make you cough and splutter. So be careful. Squeeze in some garlic, cook for a few seconds and throw in your sliced (cultivated) mushrooms. Add pepper and salt.

If you turn off the heat now and keep stirring the mushrooms so that they absorb all the liquid, you will have a dish that displays the delicate taste of the fungus at its best. Put the mushrooms in a serving dish, allow them to cool, sprinkle over some extra virgin olive oil when quite cold, and garnish the dish with some chopped parsley or parsley fronds.

If you leave the heat on and stir the mushrooms, you will notice that in many cases, especially when the cultivated mushrooms are fresh, they will give out some liquid. Now is a good time to pour off this liquid into a bowl. Add to it some granular mustard. Mix well and return the mustardy liquid to the mushrooms as their sauce.

Should you decide to carry on cooking until the liquid given out by the mushrooms has evaporated, the mushrooms will shrink in size and take on yet another taste. This is the kind to serve on toast or crisp fried bread.

You may feel like adding things to make mushrooms your own special dish, at whatever stage you turn off the heat. You might add stoned olives, cooked peppers, small pieces of orange or lemon peel, paprika, other herbs and spices, etc., etc.

* * *

Newcomers to dockland, avocado pears are best bought when rock hard before they ripen to a stage when shoppers begin to squish and bruise them to see if they are ready. Immediately they have some "give" when pressed, they should be ready. The taste varies somewhat from one variety to another. I tend to favour the knobbly kind that are on the smaller side. Simply cut them through from the pointed to rounded end, give the top and bottom a twist and they will separate into halves, one half retaining the pip. Extract this with the point of a knife blade. The pear halves are now ready to eat in their half skin with the cavity full of some or other filling, or when the skin has been peeled off and the yellow flesh sliced.

AVOCADOS AND FILLINGS

You will need:
Ripe avocado pears
Fillings

One of the best fillings is the simplest, of just adding oil and vinegar to the cavity and then milling over some black pepper. Oil, chopped onion and chilli sauce is another filling. Crisply fried bacon bits with or without a vinaigrette is excellent. Prawns with a dressing of mayonnaise mixed with tomato paste or ketchup is the restaurant favourite. Then you might consider any of the following mixtures to fill the inviting cavity where the pip once rested: hummus with added lemon juice, fish paté, horseradish minced up with hard boiled egg, chopped hard boiled egg with butter and anchovy essence, smoked cod's roe mashed up with a little oil and lemon juice, grated vegetables, and so on and so on.

* * *

Here is an hors d'oeuvre or main vegetable dish of Mediterranean origin. It appears on the menu of most Greek and Middle Eastern restaurants and was no doubt consumed by the colourful lascars and other Mediterranean sailors who came to the docks. It may be eaten alone with a fork, but is best put on to pieces of warm pitta (Arab) bread or scooped out of a dish with taco chips. It can be used as a dip (page 57) at a party, using pitta bread or chips of some sort, but can spill and make the floor messy if made too thin. So, if wanted for a stand-up do, make it thicker. One of its greatest assets, besides being delicious, is that it is economical and easy to make. Moreover, what you do not need right away can be frozen in the quantities needed for future use. When you have made it once, you will wonder why you ever bought it from the shops.

HUMMUS

For this you will need:
Dried chickpeas (or cooked from a jar or can)
Tahini paste from a jar (or cheaper peanut butter)
Lemon juice
Garlic
Pepper and salt
Oil

Soak dried chickpeas overnight. A 500g. packet will make a goodly quantity. Cover generously with cold water and boil them until tender. Depending upon how old and dry they are, this can take an hour to an hour and a half, or perhaps more. Ladle off the scum that may rise to the surface when the water starts to boil. When the chickpeas are soft (they are always fairly firm, even when cooked) put them through a food mill or liquidiser. For speed use cooked chickpeas from a jar or can, but bought in this way they will be more expensive. At this stage you can decide upon a smooth paste or a slightly rougher one. I use the medium disc of my hand-operated food mill to give the hummus a bit of bite. Now stir in say a tablespoon of tahini paste. This may well have separated out in its jar, so give it a stir first. The same amount of peanut butter will do almost as well, and it is easier to obtain. Add plenty of pepper and salt, the juice of a lemon, a crushed garlic clove or two (best squeezed through a garlic press) and a good slosh of vegetable or olive oil. The result may still be quite firm, so rather than add more oil to reach the desired consistency, put in some of the water in which the chickpeas were boiled. The rest of the cooking water could be added to a soup or used to cook another vegetable. When allowed to cool, the cooking water will appear to be quite viscous.

You can eat the hummus right away, but it is better if left for a while for the garlic taste to spread throughout the mixture. Then it is time to test again. It might need more salt, garlic, oil or lemon juice.

* * *

Beans were used in dockland past on their own as a vegetable or in stews. This is a simple dish with which to start a meal. Make sure to cook more red kidney beans than necessary. Those left over may then be added to soups, mixed salads, stews or turned into chilli con carne. When prepared (well beforehand, if wanted), this economical first course will decorate the table in a most inviting way.

RED BEANS AND HOT DRESSING

For this you will need:
Red kidney beans (dried or from a can or jar)
Onion
Parsley
Vinaigrette

Soak red kidney beans overnight or for longer. Then, depending on their age (dryness), boil them for 35 minutes or more (sometimes much more) until firm, yet soft enough to enjoy. Make sure that when cooking the beans for the first 10 minutes that the water boils vigorously. This is to ensure that noxious toxins are eliminated. So never slow-cook red kidney beans unless they have first been submitted to this initial 10 minutes of vigorous boiling.

Of course you can buy cooked beans in a can or jar, but this is a much more expensive way of using them, and less eco-friendly.

Drain the beans and present them cold as individual servings.

Chop onions finely and distribute the pieces over the beans. Now sprinkle chopped parsley over the top.

Make up your dressing of a vinaigrette (page 54), possibly adding mustard and/or chopped chillies or chilli sauce, and heat it up. When about to eat, pour or ladle some of the dressing over each serving. Do this as your fellow diners watch so that they can determine the right amount, or put the hot vinaigrette into a jug and allow your eaters to serve themselves.

As hot vinaigrette is inclined to separate, it will need to be stirred before each serving. So place a wooden spoon in either saucepan or jug.

NOTE: To add extra colours, tastes and textures, you could use several kinds of beans in the presentation. But as different varieties of beans take different times to cook, there will be much more work to do, unless, of course, you buy them already cooked in can or jar.

Tarragon vinegar is an improvement on wine vinegar for this bean dish.

***

Rice was used in dockland past mainly for rice pudding (page 116). It was also added to soups and stews. Rice salad does sound a bit boring. But with a bit of imagination it can be turned into one of the very best of dishes as a first course or main one for vegetarians. Both like it in equal measure. A large bowl of this salad will make a summer's day feast - and be economical and easy to prepare.

You could boil rice especially for it, but why not cook more than will be wanted for, say, a curry or whatever you normally eat with rice. Then you could start to prepare the following day's salad right away with the surplus.

RICE SALAD

For this you will need:
Rice
Oil
Vinegar (or lemon juice)
Pepper and salt
Various additions

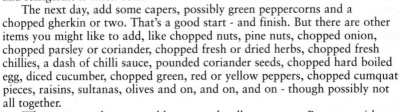

Let us presume that you have cooked more boiled rice than wanted for a meal. Put what is left over in a bowl and add oil, vinegar (or lemon juice), pepper and salt. Give it a good stir. If the rice is still hot or warm, so much the better. Cover the bowl and refrigerate it when cold.

The next day, add some capers, possibly green peppercorns and a chopped gherkin or two. That's a good start - and finish. But there are other items you might like to add, like chopped nuts, pine nuts, chopped onion, chopped parsley or coriander, chopped fresh or dried herbs, chopped fresh chillies, a dash of chilli sauce, pounded coriander seeds, chopped hard boiled egg, diced cucumber, chopped green, red or yellow peppers, chopped cumquat pieces, raisins, sultanas, olives and on, and on, and on - though possibly not all together.

Whatever you choose to add, you can hardly go wrong. But start with a simple few ingredients - like capers and chopped gherkins. These give the salad some 'bite'. Nuts and peppers will give it added colour and texture.

From plain and simple rice you will have made a delicious salad. For a main course, decorate it with halved hard-boiled eggs, tomato quarters, sardines or anchovies. Add a few black olives to delight the eye.

To elevate the salad to a much higher plane, skin a small knob of fresh ginger root. Cut this up as finely as you can and add it.

* * *

Plain scrambled eggs, made with eggs and milk and served on bread toasted in front of the grate, was a common dish in old dockland. Now, omelettes are more popular, and they can be filled with various ingredients to make them more versatile.

OMELETTES

For these you will need:
Eggs
Butter
Pepper and salt
Additions if desired

Break two
eggs into a
bowl, whisk
them up with a
fork. Add pepper
and salt. Whisk again.
Heat a lump of butter in a
frying pan until it melts but not
browns, making sure that the bottom
and edges of the pan have been
covered with the melted butter, and pour the surplus into the bowl with the eggs. Add the beaten egg to the pan and turn the pan until all the bottom has been coated with beaten egg. As it cooks, draw in the cooked egg to the centre, allowing any uncooked egg to take its place. Continue this until the omelette is cooked yet still moist. Fold the omelette over and slide it on to a plate.

Add cooked mushrooms to the mixture or fold the omelette around some.

Cook some trimmed sorrel or spinach leaves in the butter until they turn colour, add the beaten egg, stir and continue.

Mix cooked tomatoes in with the egg.

Mix in chopped, cooked green beans or cooked broad beans.

Chopped fresh herbs added to the beaten egg make a wonderful omelette. The combination of parsley and chives is about the best. Chopped tarragon is good.

Cooked peas are excellent and colourful.

For Spanish omelette, see later.

***

VEGETABLES ALONE

I have mentioned that vegetarians, if there were any, lay thin on the ground in the days of old dockland. It is a different matter today. With so many meat scares, there is a strong movement, especially with the young, towards vegetarianism. Although there are many other vegetarian dishes in this book, the following are especially for them.

Pease pudding is synonymous with dockland cooking. "Pease pudding hot, pease pudding cold, pease pudding in the pot nine days old" tells us that it is eaten hot and cold and lasts well without going off (I found that it became mouldy after five days of a longevity test in a pot and in warm conditions. So refrigerate it, or as they did in dockland past, put it in the larder). There is hardly a person in the East End who does not drool at the very thought of this dish. Pease pudding (often made by the butcher) was eaten especially with saveloys and faggots. It is also very much a dockland dish inasmuch as it takes a long time to cook, so was ideal when the kitchen range was alight for much of the time. I can do no more than start by giving a recipe directly from a docklander who has made and eaten it all her life.

PEASE PUDDING

For this you will need:
Split peas
Margarine or butter
Eggs, sometimes
Pepper and salt

"Soak split peas overnight. Put them in a cloth and boil until soft. Mash with margarine, pepper and salt."
That is the dockland recipe at its simplest.

The following is a more detailed recipe: Soak split peas overnight or for 24 hours, adding a little bicarbonate of soda. Tie the peas loosely in a clean cloth (see note No. 1) and boil for 2 1/4 hours. Mash them up with butter, 2 beaten eggs, pepper and salt. Now tie tightly in a clean floured cloth and boil again for another hour. Put the pease pudding in a pot and serve hot or cold.

Bacon fat is sometimes added, and the mixture even incorporated into dumpling mix (page 72).

Pease pudding was often made in the same pot when boiling pork, beef or mutton.

NOTES: No. 1. This is best contrived by placing a 2'x 2' clean cloth in a colander into which you tip the soaked peas. Rest the colander above a bowl. Twist the opposing corners of the cloth and tie above securely. After the 2 1/2 hours, drain the bag of cooked peas. Do this by suspending the bag over the sink, bowl or other container until no water drips from it. Tip the contents of the bag back into the dry saucepan and mash as directed above. In the meantime, wash out the cloth and return it to the colander above a bowl, giving the upper surface a dusting of flour. Return the mashed peas to the cloth in the colander and tie up as before. Boil again as directed.

Like many a true dockland dish, the result is both economical and filling. A 500 gram packet of green split peas will make a formidable dish.

To put a trivet beneath the bag of peas as they boil will reduce the bumping noise. Add boiling water to the saucepan as necessary.

Pease pudding sandwiches were very popular in dockland.

* * *

Potatoes have formed a staple food for northern Europeans almost since the day they were introduced from South America in the mid 1500s. They have been a vital ingredient of dockland cooking.

We start with plain "mash". It is always wise to make much more mashed potato than you want for the meal as cold mash can be used to thicken soups and in many other ways, like in corned beef hash and fish cakes. The extraordinary thing about mashed potato is that it is seldom considered as a main course. Perhaps this is because there seem to have been so few variations of it. Although dockland mash has seldom been more than boiled potato mashed up, let us start with the plain, popular, and possibly the most delicious version. Later, in Mash Variations, we think about some modern ways of presenting the mashed tuber, ones that make the dish much more special.

PLAIN AND DELICIOUS MASHED POTATO

For this you will need:
Potatoes
Butter
Milk
Pepper and salt

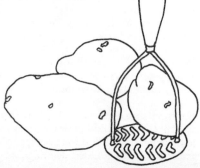

Peel potatoes, cutting large ones into half so that all are about the same size. Put them in cold, salted water, bring to the boil and cook until they are soft enough to mash. Depending on the type of potato chosen, this could take perhaps from 10 to 20 minutes or more. Watch them carefully, prodding them with the point of a knife until they are ready. Cloudy water may give an indication when this time has arrived.

Pour off and keep the water for soup or stock and, when quite dry, mash them with a fork, potato masher or in a food mill.

Now put in a good sized lump of butter and plenty of pepper and salt. Cover the butter with mashed potato and it will soon melt. Mash again. Add milk. You will be surprised how much of it will be absorbed.

If you are going to eat the mash as mash, add enough milk to form the consistency you like. If the potato is to be used to cover a pie (as in shepherd's or cottage pie) add only a very little milk, and less butter, too. If you are going to put the mash into an ovenproof dish and place it in a hot oven for it to rise, like a soufflé, add a lot of milk - enough to make it sloshy. In this case, the potato will rise, be transformed in taste, form a brown crust on top, and keep hot in the oven for some time without spoiling.

* * *

Now let us go on to variations probably never heard of in old dockland.

MASH VARIATIONS

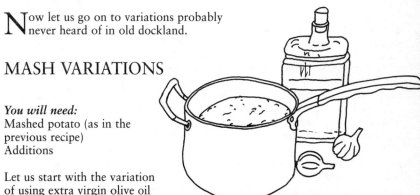

You will need:
Mashed potato (as in the previous recipe)
Additions

Let us start with the variation of using extra virgin olive oil instead of butter. You might then like to press a garlic clove into the result. Mix it in thoroughly.

Capers and chopped-up olives are Mediterranean-type additions.

A finely chopped onion will enliven and sometimes astound the taste buds on your tongue. Finely chopped chives add a more delicate onion taste. The Dutch like to add cooked green vegetables to mashed potato. Try peas.

Perhaps add grated cheese (Parmesan is good) or horseradish sauce.

Crushed seeds, like pepper, coriander and cumin are possibilities. A chopped fresh herb is another - or mixed herbs.

Turmeric powder, if dissolved in a little water, will make the mash yellow and alter its taste. But don't add too much of it. Expensive saffron, if soaked in hot water for a while, will do the same.

Should you be presenting any of these delicious concoctions as a vegetarian main dish, consider making up balls of the mash and rolling them in flour before frying or deep-frying them. When golden brown, sprinkle over some chopped parsley or coriander before serving.

* * *

This Jewish dockland method is one of the quickest, easiest, most economical and delicious ways of cooking potatoes. So the recipe is very useful if you have just reached home late, nothing is immediately available to eat, and you are hungry. Use these potato pancakes on their own, with other vegetables, with fried eggs, bacon, chops, hamburgers, cold meats, corned beef or fish fingers, etc.

POTATO PANCAKES

For these you will need:
Potatoes
Pepper and salt
Oil, dripping or oil and butter
Onion (optional)

Heat a generous quantity of olive oil, cooking oil, or a mixture of oil and butter in a frying pan. Now, on to a plate or into a bowl grate well washed potatoes. It is not necessary to peel them. Add pepper and salt and a little grated onion if desired. Do not at this stage delay or the potatoes will discolour. Spoon the mixture into the hot oil and flatten into small, thin pancakes. Make absolutely sure that each is separated from its neighbours. Cook until brown beneath and then turn them over until glowing brown on both sides. Drain the oil from each and, if thought necessary, place on kitchen paper to drain further.

Serve with what you will.

* * *

Here is a dish for vegetarians on its own or as a vegetable to accompany any meat, such as faggots, chicken, lamb, pork, game or beef.

POTATOES AND ONIONS BAKED IN MILK

For this you will need:
Potatoes
Onions
Pepper and salt
Milk, butter

Take a fairly shallow iron or ovenproof
crockery dish and line the bottom of it with a layer of peeled, thinly sliced
potatoes. Cover this with a layer of sliced onions, giving them a good dusting
of salt and pepper. Finally add a top layer of sliced potatoes. Alternatively,
the potatoes and onions may be overlapped in rows - scallop shaped or even
put in higgledy-piggledy. Place some lumps of butter all over and add milk to
almost cover the top layer of potatoes. Do not cover.

Bake the dish in a medium to hot oven until the vegetables are cooked.
This could take an hour to an hour and a half - depending on the oven heat,
the position in the oven, thickness of dish, type of potatoes and all those
other variables that go to make timing so imprecise. You will find that the
potatoes will absorb most, if not all of the milk. The dish will be ready when
the top is crisp and brown, the inside soft and most of the liquid absorbed.

Pork chops, possibly previously marinated in vinaigrette and whole
coriander seeds, could bake at the same time.

* * *

Bubble and squeak, or just bubble, has always been a real dockland
favourite in both home and in cafes and dining rooms.

BUBBLE AND SQUEAK

For this you will need:
Mashed potato
A cooked green vegetable, usually cabbage
Dripping
Pepper and salt

Take mashed potatoes or broken up cold boiled
potatoes, and cooked greens. In dockland, cabbage is
by far the most popular. Brussels sprouts are also used. Stir them together
with pepper and salt and fry the mixture in dripping (for preference, though
fats or oils will do almost as well) until browning top and bottom.

* * *

Cold boiled potatoes fried with onions has always been a dockland favourite mixture. It will go excellently with sausages, hamburgers, fish fingers, chops, eggs, cold meats and much else.

It can be made also with sliced, raw, peeled potatoes and sliced onions if put into a lidded pan with some fat or oil and cooked slowly in its own steam, then to brown with the lid taken off. This is the way with an omelette in Spain, as I found out just after WW2 when stopping in a small village in the Costa Brava (high rise had yet to appear on the scene). A café owner, with nothing else to offer, cooked a Spanish omelette for me as above, adding beaten eggs to the potatoes and onion just cooked, to hold it together and form a grand dish.

FRIED POTATOES AND ONIONS, AND SPANISH OMELETTE

You will need:
Potatoes
Onions
Olive oil, other oil, fat or dripping
Pepper and salt
Eggs for the Spanish omelette

For the mixed vegetable,
fry sliced, boiled potatoes and sliced onions until brown, remembering to add pepper and salt.

For the Spanish omelette,
cut up well-washed, peeled potatoes into smallish pieces. Throw the pieces into a frying pan that has a lid (electric frying pans are ideal) with some olive oil and plenty of pepper and salt.

Now skin some onions and chop these up, adding them to the potatoes. Stir the pieces so that each is coated with oil. Put on the lid and cook slowly, stirring occasionally, until the vegetables are soft.

Now take off the lid and add beaten eggs with pepper and salt. Put on the lid once more and slowly cook the omelette through.

You can turn or toss the omelette if you like. The result should be moist, not dry.

* * *

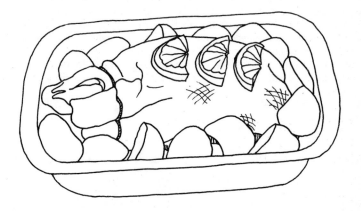

R oast potatoes with roast meat are a dockland and almost universal favourite dish. They even make a wonderful treat if cooked on their own. The results will vary somewhat depending on the variety of potatoes and oil or fat used. But that does not matter much, as they will be delicious almost every time with their golden, crisp outsides and soft centres. Dripping helps to make the best.

ROAST POTATOES

You will need:
Potatoes
Dripping or oil
Pepper and salt

Peel enough potatoes to satisfy the appetites of everyone. Cut the potatoes into pieces about the same size and wash them well. Boil for 10 minutes, coat them completely with olive oil or cooking oil, or, the best, melted dripping (see Dripping on page 118). Pepper and salt them. They will be ready in an hour or more or when the meat is cooked. There will be no need to baste or worry about them in the oven.

* * *

Cauliflower cheese is a favourite in old and new dockland with adults and children, meat eaters and vegetarians. It can be made well before it is wanted at the table. Just prepare it and leave it in the oven until about an hour before wanted, and then turn on the heat. It is not too hard to make, and any left over can be heated up the next day or even the day after. There is a snag, however. Although the smell of cooking cabbage was rife in dockland kitchens past, boiling the cauliflower to soften it does make a rather nasty smell. So ventilate the kitchen as much as possible. Should the smell persist and you want to disguise it, put some real ground coffee in a saucepan, heat it up until a light smoke is created and wander around with the perfuming pan.

CAULIFLOWER CHEESE

For this you will need:
Cauliflower
The ingredients for a white sauce (see White Sauce on page 49)
Dijon mustard
Grated cheddar cheese or the like
Paprika

Trim off the leaves and much of the stem of a cauliflower (or two if small). In about 1" of water boil/steam these until it is easy to stick the point of a knife into the stem. Check the water occasionally to make sure it has not boiled away. Strain the cauliflower, retaining the water for the sauce. Put the cooked cauliflower into a shallow ovenproof dish and cut it up into small pieces. Spread them out evenly.

Now make a white sauce (see White Sauce on page 49), using milk and some or all of the water in which you cooked the cauliflower, and add grated cheese and Dijon mustard. Pour this over the cauliflower pieces until they are quite coated. Sprinkle paprika powder over it all for colour, and place the dish in the oven to cook right away or later. Bake the Cauliflower Cheese in a hottish oven until the upper surface begins to brown and the sauce bubbles.

NOTE: Try to make more sauce than you need. It could start a cream soup or enhance an existing one.

If you use grated cheese in your cooking, consider grating much more than you need for a particular dish, then bag up and refrigerate the remainder for future use.

***

For vegetarians or others, this dish was given to me in a restaurant when travelling through the Loire in the 1950s. Serve it as a first or main course, snack, light lunch or side dish. It is tasty and, having different colours, temperatures and textures, a delight to see and eat. But be careful not to burn your mouth. Fried breadcrumbs can become very hot.

CAULIFLOWER WITH GARLIC AND FRIED BREADCRUMBS

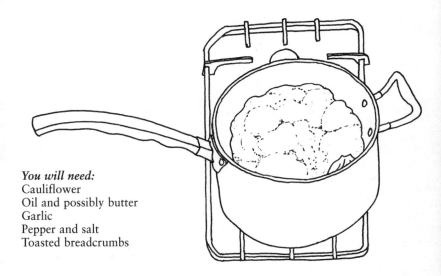

You will need:
Cauliflower
Oil and possibly butter
Garlic
Pepper and salt
Toasted breadcrumbs

Trim off and discard the leaves from a large cauliflower and steam/boil the flower part in a large, lidded saucepan in an inch or so of water for about 20 minutes - until, that is, the flowers and core are soft when prodded with a pointed knife or skewer. There will be an unpleasant smell when boiling the vegetable, so ventilate the kitchen.

In a pan, fry plenty of crushed garlic in oil, or oil and butter. When the garlic begins to turn colour, add the drained cauliflower (retaining the water for soup) and cut it into small florets, including the stem pieces if you feel like it. Add salt and pepper.

Turn the cauliflower around to be coated with oil and garlic. As this continues to cook, fry some toasted breadcrumbs in oil and butter until they become a deeper golden colour. They will also need pepper and salt. To cook the crumbs successfully, you will have to turn them over all the time, otherwise they will burn. Serve the cauliflower pieces covered with the scorchingly hot crumbs.

* * *

Although cabbage was the dockland favourite, Brussels sprouts were popular as well.

First select your Brussels sprouts. They vary a lot in taste from the bland to the deliciously nutty. As far as I can see, you will get no indication of their taste by inspecting them on the supermarket shelf or market stall.

They are best eaten in the cold of winter. In the springtime they start to enlarge and become unpleasant to eat. As a boy, we never gathered them from the kitchen garden until they had been subjected to a frost, though I have since eaten excellent sprouts before the arrival of cold weather.

Look at the base of the sprouts. Freshly picked ones will have a clean, whitish base where they have been broken or cut from their parent stem. The longer they have been offered for sale, the darker and drier this base will be.

Aim for small, tight sprouts with clean outer leaves. If only those available are bruised and/or the cut dark and dirty, it will be necessary to trim off the base with a knife and peel off the outer leaves. The sprouts will then be ready to cook. If the outer leaves are yellowing, do not buy them. Boil more than you need so that any remaining can be fried for a dish the next day - which is when they change taste and are just as delicious, if not more so.

BRUSSELS SPROUTS BOILED WITH BUTTER, THEN FRIED

You will need:
Brussels sprouts
Salt and pepper
Butter and/or oil
Garlic for the frying part

Into salted boiling water throw the trimmed sprouts. Bring the water back to the boil and time the cooking for 5 minutes exactly. They will then be cooked, firm and at their very best. Strain the cooked sprouts and return them to the pan so that any remaining water will evaporate.

Now add a good lump of butter and some salt and pepper. Toss the sprouts around until the butter has melted and coated them. Serve immediately.

If possible, retain enough sprouts to fry the following day. Then put them into a frying pan with a little oil, or oil and butter, with some pressed garlic. You might like to add a little more salt and pepper. Fry the sprouts until their outer leaves are brown and crisp, by which time the smell, with the added garlic, will be delicious. Serve.

* * *

Here is a modern dockland dish that makes a fine first course or vegetarian's main course. For either it will need plenty of crusty bread on the table with which to sop up the juices. The tomatoes can be grilled or, more slowly, baked in the oven with another dish. It is a great culinary treat, but to be so, the tomatoes must be well cooked through.

CLASSIC GRILLED TOMATOES

You will need:
Tomatoes
Olive oil
Garlic
Pepper and salt
A dried or fresh herb of
your choice
Toasted breadcrumbs

Halve tomatoes and scoop out some of the flesh to make a cavity. Place the halves in a pan, arranging the scooped-out flesh beneath and around them. Now pour olive oil into the cavities and into each press a little garlic. Add pepper and salt, and over the top sprinkle some fresh or dried herb - like parsley, sage or any other that you particularly like. Now cover each half with toasted breadcrumbs.

Grill or oven-cook the tomatoes until the cell structure has broken down and the juices have started to leak into the pan. Serve them sizzling hot with crusty, French-style bread to sop up the juices.

* * *

Those in dockland of old certainly missed out on dishes like this, as peppers are a comparatively new introduction. The following dish is very simple to make and acts as a first course that can be made well beforehand and put on the table, or served hot. It is primarily a simple vegetable but when peeled prawns or any fresh shellfish from the shrimp and winkle man are added, it immediately becomes a much more substantial dish.

FRIED PEPPERS, AND MORE

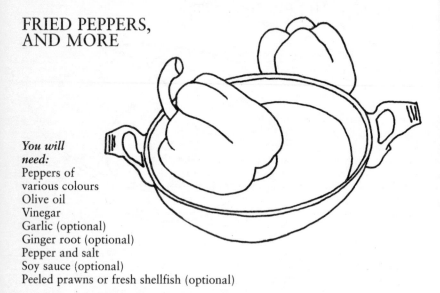

You will need:
Peppers of
various colours
Olive oil
Vinegar
Garlic (optional)
Ginger root (optional)
Pepper and salt
Soy sauce (optional)
Peeled prawns or fresh shellfish (optional)

Slice peppers of various colours in half from stem to point. Tear out the stems and discard them. Slice the flesh into lengthwise strips and divide these. Put oil in a pan with some pressed garlic and/or very finely peeled and chopped fresh ginger root. Add the peppers, a dash of vinegar and some pepper and salt. Cover it all with a lid and cook, stirring occasionally until the peppers are soft. Take away the lid, raise the heat a bit and fry the peppers until they are beginning to brown. Tip the peppers into a serving dish and, when cold, add a little best olive oil. Test for salt and pepper. That is the first dish.

At the stage when the pepper pieces are beginning to brown, it is optional to add a little soy sauce. Then, if a grander dish is wanted, add peeled prawns or some other cooked shellfish, like beheaded and tailed small shrimps, whelks out of their shells, scallops, cockles (fresh and not in brine), etc. Stir these in so that they are coated with the juices, but do not cook them further.

***

SAUCES

The word "sauces" conjours up a picture of French chefs, with pencil-thin moustaches, adding a soupçon of this, that and the other to sauces of great elegance. The traditional and imaginative sauces that follow err on the simple side.

Custard, made with custard powder, hot milk and sugar, is and was the almost obligatory sauce for pies, tarts, sweet puddings, stewed apple, stewed fruit, tinned fruit and almost everything else constituting a dockland pudding. But there were really three dockland custards. The one of old was made from eggs and milk for sauce, also to be eaten on its own in a cup. Then there comes the simple custard powder variety. Finally there is the one often given to the sickly, baked with eggs and milk.

CUSTARDS AND BREAD AND BUTTER PUDDING

For the old variety of custard you will need:
Egg yolks
Sugar
Milk
Flavouring, such as bay leaf or vanilla

Beat 3 egg yolks (4 for the custard to set firmly). Add 3/4 of a pint of hot, but not boiling milk, heated up with a bay leaf or two if that has been used for the flavour. Put this mixture into a jug and stand the jug in a saucepan of warm water. Heat the water slowly on the hob or over a low flame, stirring the custard until it thickens. Now add 1oz. of white sugar, stirring it in. At the same time include vanilla essence if that is your choice of flavouring.

For the more recent variety of custard you will need:
Custard powder from a tin
Sugar
Milk

Place a tablespoon of custard powder in a basin with the same amount of sugar. Make a paste of it with a little milk from a pint. Bring the rest of the pint to the boil (just) and add it to the paste, stirring all the time. Return the resultant custard to the saucepan and, stirring all the time, boil it slowly until it thickens.

For the baked custard you will need:
Eggs
Milk
Salt
Sugar
Flavouring, such as nutmeg

Beat up 2 eggs, with the yolks only from two more. Add a pint of milk and a pinch of salt. Put the mixture into a greased pie dish and grate nutmeg over it. Bake in a medium oven for about an hour.

There was another old dockland variety of baked custard. This was a savoury edition with stock taking the place of milk. Pepper and salt was added, and parsley took the place of sugar. There was no additional flavouring.

For Bread and Butter Pudding you will need:
Bread and butter
Milk
Eggs
Sugar
Sultanas and/or currants

Butter, say 6 slices of white bread and cut off and discard the crusts. Cut the slices into smallish squares. Butter a pie dish and in it place alternate layers of the bread pieces and sultanas. Do not fill the dish much over half way up.

Make a custard by whisking 2 eggs with a dessertspoon of sugar. To this add a pint of milk. Whisk again. Pour the mixture over the bread to cover it, and allow the liquid to settle and soak into the bread for around an hour. With the oven on low heat, bake the pudding for about an hour.

***

Parsley sauce and custard are the great sauces of dockland. Parsley sauce is the sauce of eel and pie shops.

PARSLEY SAUCE

Make a white sauce as below and add freshly chopped parsley.

* * *

Now we come to make a white sauce. And very simple it is. It is the basis for parsley sauce (above), almost all cream soups, and delicate sauces to pour over vegetable dishes. So it is a very important sauce in dockland past and present.

WHITE SAUCE

You will need:
Butter
Plain flour
Pepper and salt
Milk, milk and water,
or milk and stock

Put a saucepan over a moderate heat source and throw in a good lump of butter. Allow it to melt, but not burn or brown. Then add about the same volume, or more, of plain flour. Stir the flour into the melted butter. The result may be soft and bubbling or rather dry. Add plenty of pepper and salt. Now add liquid in the form of milk, milk and water, or milk and stock. How much liquid should you add? Well, experience will tell you, but, at a guess, try about ten times the amount of solids. Now immediately whisk the liquid to eliminate any lumps and keep whisking it as it heats through and thickens. If it is too thick, add more liquid. If it is too liquid, cook it slowly until some of the liquid evaporates. That is the white sauce, and, depending on the stock used, it will be bland or tasty.

Stir in freshly chopped parsley to make a parsley sauce.

I always add some Dijon mustard to my white sauces, and sometimes a little grated cheese. The taste of both of these will be lost in the overall flavour of the sauce but they will definitely enhance it.

You will notice that most whisks are rounded and the bottoms of most saucepans are right angled. So as you whisk and stir the sauce there will be a section that will stick, burn and possibly spoil it. So as you whisk, use a spoon to run around the inside of the bottom of the saucepan to bring the untouched mixture back into the sauce.

* * *

We will use this basic white sauce for making cream soups when we get to the soup section. Now is the time to consider what might be added to white sauce to create flavoursome coatings for vegetables, and sometimes fish or meat.

WHITE SAUCES FOR VEGETABLES - AND MUCH ELSE

You will need the basic white sauce as above:
If needing a white sauce for whatever vegetable, fish or meat you are cooking, use the liquid in which you cooked the said vegetable, fish or meat as part liquid for your sauce.

Plain white or parsley sauces go well with boiled leeks, potatoes, Brussels sprouts, carrots, parsnips, broccoli, cauliflower, boiled fish or halved hard-boiled eggs.

White sauce for boiled meat, especially mutton (hogget for preference), often has capers added to make a caper sauce.

A whole boiled chicken or chicken pieces, when cool and coated with a white tarragon or parsley sauce, is delicious if served cold when the sauce has set.

Saffron, when soaked in hot water and added to a white sauce, can be used on many a dish. Other fresh herbs than those mentioned above may also be added to it.

Curry powder if whisked into a little water to eliminate lumps and added to a white sauce can be used over many a vegetable, fish or eggs.

Chopped hard boiled eggs added to white sauce will coat many a vegetable or fish course to enhance both taste and looks.

Add more cheese to make a cheese sauce.

White sauces improve the presentation and taste of many a dish that you have in mind to serve.

***

The following sauce is one of the most versatile and delicious. It was not an old dockland sauce, as it needs to be cooked in quantity, bagged in meal-size portions, and stored in the freezer or freezing compartment of the refrigerator until wanted. For a family with children it is a godsend.

BASIC MEAT SAUCE

You will need:
Ground minced beef
Olive oil or other cooking oil
Salt and pepper
Concentrated tomato paste
Sugar
Vinegar
Paprika
Cornflour

Because the cooking time will take 3-4-5 hours, you might just as well make a large quantity at one time. Use some of the meat sauce for a dish right away, perhaps for spaghetti, and bag up the rest later when it is cold. Use transparent freezer bags, roll down the tops, spoon in the sauce, squeeze out any air and tie a knot in each bag to seal it. Then put the squishy bags in the freezing compartment of your refrigerator or deep freeze for future use.

Buy about 3 pounds of ground minced beef. Put it in a large saucepan with a generous amount of olive oil or oil of your choice (oil improves the sauce and gives a gloss to such dishes as spaghetti) and pepper and salt. Cook this until the mince has changed colour to brown and the larger lumps have been broken up (use a potato masher for this). In a big bowl put the contents of two 400g. cans of concentrated tomato paste, washing out the cans with water and adding this to the sauce to make sure there is no waste. Add water to about 5 or more times the volume of the paste. Pour in a slosh of vinegar (wine vinegar for preference) and, say a heaped teaspoon of sugar. Now add some paprika (for colour as much as anything) and whisk up the mixture until it becomes a smooth liquid containing no lumps. Add this to the meat. You may need more water, as the mixture should now have the thickness of thin cream. Wash out the bowl with water and add this to the sauce, again to avoid waste. Possibly use a potato masher once more to break up any lumps of mince in the mixture.

Bring the meat sauce to the boil and turn down the heat until it simmers slowly and gives off steam. Rest the lid on the pan, leaving a gap to allow moisture to escape in the form of steam. The lid will prevent the sauce from splashing out on to the top of the stove. Allow the sauce to cook for 3-5 hours, by which time the level in the saucepan will have dropped by possibly an inch and the sauce acquired a wonderful and appetising smell. Test it for pepper and salt. It might even need more vinegar and/or sugar. Adjust as you think necessary.

Now, depending on the amount of sauce being made, put about two or three heaped dessert spoons of cornflour in a bowl and add cold water to it until a liquid has been formed. Stir this into the hot sauce, whisking it as you do so, to make sure that no lumps form. Cook for a few minutes longer until the sauce thickens. Then move the pot from the heat.

Stir it all together. Use some sauce right away if wanted, and allow the rest to cool down, possibly overnight. Stir the sauce again so that any oil on the surface is mixed evenly throughout the blend, and bag it up in the quantities desired. Put them in the freezer.

Among the dishes with which you might incorporate this sauce are: Spaghetti with Meat Sauce (page 73), Pop's Pasta (page 75), Cottage and Shepherd's Pie (page 89), Chilli con Carne (page 88) and Curried Mince and Peas (page 91).

***

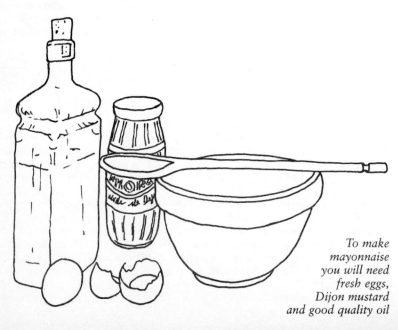

To make mayonnaise you will need fresh eggs, Dijon mustard and good quality oil

Of course it is possible to buy mayonnaise in a glass jar at the supermarket or dockland grocery shop, and perfectly all right it will be. But to make your own, for perhaps a sauce for cold chicken or egg mayonnaise, is well worthwhile. And it is easy. Moreover, if you do make your own, people seem to think you know what you are about in the kitchen. But in making mayonnaise there is a vital point to remember, and it is that the eggs you use must be from a natural and hygienic source where the chickens roam in the farmyard or countryside scratching and pecking for their food. And the eggs must be very fresh. The reason for this is that battery produced eggs, even when fresh, may contain salmonella.

MAYONNAISE

You will need:
Fresh egg(s)
Dijon mustard
Oil

Separate the yolk from the white of a raw, fresh egg. Do this by cracking around the 'waist' of the shell with the back of a knife, then opening the egg when it is upright and allowing the white to fall away. Then gently tip the yolk back to the empty half shell, arranging for any remaining white to fall away. (The white may be saved for an omelette, meringues, mayonnaise, toast, scrambled egg or some other dish.) Another way of separating yolk from white is to break the egg into a saucer and then 'capture' the yolk in an upturned egg-cup, pouring off the white.

Put the yolk into a bowl and add to it the same volume of Dijon mustard. Stir them together. Now, very slowly, add oil of your choice, stirring around in one direction as you do so. (Olive oil will impart its distinctive taste to the mayonnaise, other, blander oils may not.) The mayonnaise will thicken and soon be ready. Some add a little water.

Any mayonnaise left over from its intended use will help go to make Mayonnaise Toast by whisking it up with an egg and milk, into which slices of bread are then soaked and fried.

***

This is one of the most used sauces and possibly the simplest. The sauce, or dressing, is combined with most green salads (though salad cream was the popular one in dockland), put on to tomatoes, cucumbers and onions, poured over slices of cold meat or brawn to make a musseau, added to cooked rice to make the start of a rice salad, used as a dip or coating for raw and cooked vegetables, put into the cavity of avocado pears, and so on and so on.

The type of oil and vinegar you decide to use when concocting vinaigrette will make a difference to the end result, as will the proportions you decide upon. The French make the simplest for their green salads, using a bland oil, like groundnut or soybean, and a little very acidic vinegar with pepper and salt.

You might choose olive oil (which even after WW2 was only to be found in the chemist shops in dockland). This imparts a very distinctive taste to the vinaigrette, especially if extra virgin olive oil is used. You might decide on half olive oil and half, or all, groundnut, soybean, rapeseed, cooking or sunflower oil. Then there are more exotic oils from which to choose, like walnut or grapeseed. But start with a plain and bland cooking oil and whatever vinegar is in the kitchen.

Be careful not to select the kind of vinegar used in dockland fish and chip shops. This non-brewed condiment is derived from mineral oils. Malt vinegar, white or coloured, is made from natural ingredients. Wine vinegar is excellent and can be made at home with wine dregs and a "mother" in a vinaigrier. So now let us get down to the simple process of making vinaigrette.

VINAIGRETTE

You will need:
Oil
Vinegar
Pepper and salt
Possible other
variations and
additions

Pour oil (say a tablespoon for a start) into a bowl and add about 1/4 of its volume of vinegar (some choose 1/3 others 1/6 or even less). Run a pinch of salt down the inside of the bowl, and to it add a shake of ground white pepper. Now, rub the salt and pepper into the oil between the back of a wooden spoon and the side of the bowl. Stir it all together until you have a blended mixture of the ingredients. That's it. If this mixture rests for a while in the bowl, stir it together again before mixing it into a green salad or adding it to cold beans, avocado pear and such. Adding it too early to a green salad will fatigue the leaves.

My own preference is to include a good pinch of powdered English mustard and another of icing sugar when mixing in the salt and pepper.

You may like to pour a "special" vinaigrette over slices of cold meat, to be served with hot potatoes. For this you could make it as above and add any, or all of the following: finely chopped onions, capers, chopped pickled gherkins or cucumbers, green peppercorns, chopped de-seeded chillies, garlic or any other spicy ingredient or herb of your choice. This elaborate cold vinaigrette is also very good when spooned over hot pork chops. Generally used cold, this vinaigrette may also be heated and, at the time of serving, poured over cold red beans, green beans, haricot, butter, mung and soy beans, etc.

* * *

When I lived in dockland in the 1960s, this sauce accompanied many a dish in the Chinese restaurants around Salmon Lane, Pennyfields and the West India Dock Road. It was so popular that many diners asked for a plate of extra sauce when ordering curried chicken wings or whatever. It is a very useful sauce in which to serve meat, fish, vegetables or eggs. Also use it as a vehicle in which to serve leftovers.

CHINESE CURRY SAUCE

You will need:
Butter
Flour
Curry powder
Five spices
Salt or soy sauce
Stock or stock cube
The Chinese would use monosodium glutamate
Gravy browning (optional)

In a bowl mix, say a level or heaped dessertspoon of curry powder, two heaped dessertspoons of plain flower, a teaspoon of five spices and some salt or soy sauce. Mix them together. In a saucepan melt a large lump of butter, and when melted, add the spice/flour mixture. Stir it around, cook for a little and then add plenty of stock or stock cube dissolved in hot water. Whisk this together and continue to cook until the sauce thickens. Adjust the thickness of the sauce by adding water or allowing it to cook for a while longer. Thinnish sauces are often the more satisfactory. Darken the sauce if desired by adding gravy browning. Test it for balance.

Add very thin slices of high quality, fat-free beef (raw or cooked), cooked chicken, just-cooked vegetables, bone-free fish, hard boiled eggs or other items. When the added ingredients are cooked or heated through, serve as a dish by itself, or with plain boiled rice.

* * *

Pasta is now almost everyone's favourite dish, be they meat eaters or vegetarians. Yet except for vermicelli and macaroni, it hardly appeared on dockland menus in the past. The most useful sauce for pasta of almost any kind is basic meat sauce (see page 51). There are many others. Here are a few.

SOME SAUCES FOR PASTA

1. Basic meat sauce (page 51).

2. Basic meat sauce to which you add a can of anchovy fillets pounded to a pulp and some capers.

3. To cooked pasta add salt, butter and garlic.

4. Pesto. You may have a lot of sweet basil leaves at hand now that pots of it are offered in many shops (re-pot the rooted pieces into larger pots of good potting compost. Water and feed regularly) to grind up with olive oil, garlic, Parmesan or pecorino cheese and pine nuts.

   Much handier, this sauce can be bought already made up in a jar or measured from a bulk pot in an Italian delicatessen. But freshly pressed garlic and a few chopped basil leaves with good olive oil, if added to the bought mixture, will enhance it no end.

5. Vegetarian sauce. Finely chop some onions and garlic. Fry them in olive oil until soft but not brown. Add chopped peppers (green, yellow or red), a can of chopped tomatoes and plenty of stoned, chopped olives (green or black). Pepper and salt it and cook to reduce to the desired consistency.

6. Mussel sauce. Steam open mussels (or use any other shellfish) and take the meat from the shells. Now cook chopped tomatoes, fresh or from a can, some pressed garlic, olive oil and pepper and salt. Cook until the desired consistency is reached and add the shellfish. Keep the shellfish in their shells if you want to spend time and have more fun when eating.

7. To cooked pasta add olive oil, chopped garlic and finely chopped de-seeded chillies. Do not forget to add salt.

* * *

Raw vegetables contain all their healthy nutrients and are good when prepared in handleable shapes to be dipped into a sauce or choice of sauces. If the vegetables have been bought from the shop or supermarket they will probably have been sprayed with all sorts of noxious substances during the growing period. This is done to have them looking good and bug-free when presented on the display shelves. Supermarkets insist upon it unless the vegetables have been organically grown (and why are there not caterpillars and slugs in these, as there are when the same vegetables are grown in any home garden?). So always give vegetables (and fruit) a good wash when you have bought them. If they come from a spray-free garden, soak them in salty water to deal with caterpillars etc., and make sure they are free of soil. These are simple and sensible measures to take.

COLD AND HOT DIP SAUCES

You will need:
Raw vegetables
Various dips

Select one or several vegetables to eat raw
with a dip or dips. Good examples are: spring
onions, cauliflower florets, strips of carrot,
celery, chicory leaves, fennel pieces, cucumber
strips, radishes, young and tender asparagus spears,
slices of green, yellow or red pepper, trimmed mange tout peas, trimmed
French beans or podded broad beans when they are young or peeled when
older (difficult to dip, so provide cocktail sticks or tooth picks).

Now for the dips:
Straightforward mayonnaise (page 53) is a good one. Bought made-up
varieties are also good. But you might like to add things to these - like chilli
sauce, oil, vinegar, tomato ketchup, de-seeded and cut-up chillies, grated
horseradish or horseradish sauce, mustard of any kind, finely chopped
gherkins, capers, chopped onions, herbs and much else.

The next main dip is vinaigrette (page 54), though this is more liable to
drip on to floor, carpet or table top. To it you could add pretty well any of
the items mentioned for mayonnaise.

Then you could use the bought cream-type cheeses or fish roe mixtures,
again to which you could add any of those previously mentioned additions.

Hummus (page 31) is another cheap and excellent base mixture that is
ripe for additions. Thick yoghurt is another.

Then there is a special hot dip for raw vegetables, made by heating oil
and butter, adding pounded anchovies and garlic, and sometimes cream.

Any of these dips may be used as a sauce for cooked globe artichokes.

***

Gravy in dockland past was surely the most popular meat sauce for the inhabitants, as it was, and is, for those living in even colder climates. Whenever a fowl or joint of beef or mutton was roasted in the oven at home or at the baker's, its fat and juices dripped to the pan beneath. Some flour was added to these 'drippings' and left to cook for a while. Then seasonings and water or stock (often with an Oxo cube) were added to form a thickish sauce, or gravy. This was sometimes, but not always strained, and served from a jug or gravy boat. And gravy is made in almost exactly the same way now.

Gravy can be made in the roasting pan when the meat has been taken out of it or in a saucepan separately. The latter method can be contrived and made ready before the meat has been cooked. This is convenient, but has the disadvantage of not incorporating all the tasty little bits that get stuck to the pan beneath a roast.

Other flavourings may be added to gravy, liked chopped mint for mint gravy (especially good with lamb), chopped fresh herbs, tomato ketchup and Worcestershire sauce, etc. Sometimes gravy browning is added to give the sauce a more inviting colour.

This brings us to the dripping pot - to me one of the most important items in a cook's armoury of culinary tricks. So see Dripping (page 118) and use the dripping and its jelly as described.

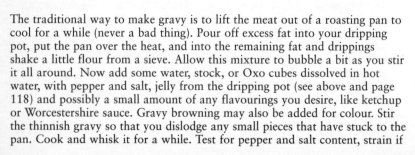

GRAVY AND OXO GRAVY

You will need:
Fat, oil or dripping
Flour
Stock, water or water and Oxo cubes
Pepper and salt
Flavourings such as tomato ketchup,
Worcestershire sauce or chopped fresh mint
or other herb
Gravy browning

The traditional way to make gravy is to lift the meat out of a roasting pan to cool for a while (never a bad thing). Pour off excess fat into your dripping pot, put the pan over the heat, and into the remaining fat and drippings shake a little flour from a sieve. Allow this mixture to bubble a bit as you stir it all around. Now add some water, stock, or Oxo cubes dissolved in hot water, with pepper and salt, jelly from the dripping pot (see above and page 118) and possibly a small amount of any flavourings you desire, like ketchup or Worcestershire sauce. Gravy browning may also be added for colour. Stir the thinnish gravy so that you dislodge any small pieces that have stuck to the pan. Cook and whisk it for a while. Test for pepper and salt content, strain if desired, and possibly add any chopped fresh herbs, if you have that in mind. Pour the lovely liquid into a jug or gravy boat and serve with the meat, potatoes or whatever.

For the easier method, and one that avoids a last-minute rush or panic, put some fat, oil or dripping into a saucepan. Heat it, sift in some flour, cook, add stock or water and dripping-pot jelly, whisk and add flavourings (perhaps Oxo cubes), gravy browning possibly, and/or chopped fresh mint or other herb. This can be kept in the saucepan, whisked, and reheated before serving with the meal in a jug or gravy boat.

***

This is a most useful sauce for pouring over and jazzing up leftover cold meat or vegetables. Its use is to spice up, or sharpen up food that would otherwise taste a bit dull and bland.

SHARP GRAVY

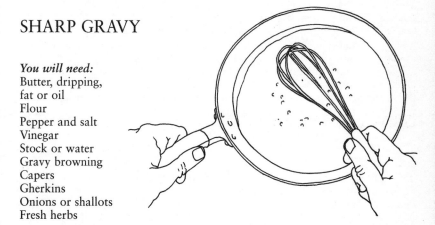

You will need:
Butter, dripping,
fat or oil
Flour
Pepper and salt
Vinegar
Stock or water
Gravy browning
Capers
Gherkins
Onions or shallots
Fresh herbs

Pour, say 1/8 of a pint of vinegar into a saucepan and boil it until it is much reduced and you can stand sniffing the fumes without discomfort. Pour it into a bowl.

In the same pan heat a good lump of butter, fat, or oil. Add flour to it until the mixture becomes a bubbly paste. Pepper and salt it. Now add the reduced vinegar, mixed with some stock. Put in a little gravy browning for colour. Now would be the right time to include dripping-pot jelly (see page 118). Whisk this mixture together to eliminate any lumps. Cook it slowly, diluting when necessary with water or stock. Taste for seasoning. The gravy will then be ready.

You may want to add some or all of the following: finely chopped gherkins, capers, onions or shallots and fresh herbs. Use on leftover meats. It is also a traditional sauce for boiled tongue.

***

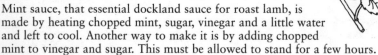

M int sauce and gravy are often served
with roast lamb or other meats. Serve
them separately or combine the two.

MINT SAUCE AND
MINT GRAVY

You will need:
Gravy
Salt and pepper
Mint
Vinegar
Sugar

Mint sauce, that essential dockland sauce for roast lamb, is
made by heating chopped mint, sugar, vinegar and a little water
and left to cool. Another way to make it is by adding chopped
mint to vinegar and sugar. This must be allowed to stand for a few hours.

For mint gravy, make a gravy in the way you please (see Gravy on page
58) and into it put plenty of finely chopped mint leaves and just a little
vinegar and sugar. Do this a minute or so before you serve the gravy so that
the heating of chopped leaves and vinegar will make them blend in well. Test
for salt and pepper content before serving the sauce in a sauceboat or directly
on to the meat.

* * *

U sually bought in a jar, some dockland cooks made
horseradish sauce from bought or home-grown roots.

HORSERADISH SAUCE

You will need:
Horseradish roots
Vinegar
Salt
Sugar
Yoghurt, optional
Hard boiled egg yolks, optional
Cream, optional

Clean the roots thoroughly by peeling and scraping them, making sure there
are no pockets of soil hiding in their many crevices. Grate the root. This will
make you cry. Or put the roots in a blender.

To the grated root add vinegar, salt and a little sugar. Store this sauce in a jar. Keep it in the refrigerator.

You might also like to add yoghurt, and/or mashed hard-boiled egg yolks to the mix. Possibly add cream at the time of serving.

* * *

Just why bread sauce seems only to appear in dockland and elsewhere at Christmas time with the turkey never fails to astound me. It is a wonderful sauce for almost all meat, fish and even vegetables. And it is easy to make.

BREAD SAUCE

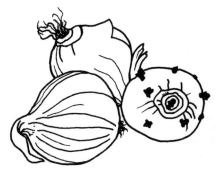

You will need:
White bread
Butter
Onions
Cloves
Milk
Pepper and salt

Start with white bread that is slightly stale. Cut off the crusts. Eat them, or bake them in the oven when it is next in use and pound or blend the crisp slices into toasted breadcrumbs. With your fingers, crumble the white 'crumb' into a bowl. Rub the larger pieces together until you have a fairly fine texture. Should you use new bread, this will be very difficult to accomplish.

Now, in a saucepan, put say half to a full pint of milk. Chop up finely one large or two small onions and add this to the milk. Skin a small onion and into it push 6 - 12 cloves. This is done more easily if you pierce the onion's skin first with a sharp instrument, like a skewer. Add the cloved onion to the milk and chopped onion. Put in plenty of pepper and salt and a good-sized lump of butter. Heat it all up until almost at the boiling point and, at that tick-over heat, continue to cook the liquid until the onion is soft. This will take longer than expected, probably from 1/4 to 1/2 an hour. Extract the cloved onion and discard it. Now add the breadcrumbs to form a sauce that is not too thick. If there are any breadcrumbs left over put them in a baking pan to be toasted in the oven with the crusts. When you do this, you may need to take out the pan to stir the bits around once or twice so that they are golden all round. Cook the sauce for a little longer, testing for salt and pepper content. Serve.

The sauce will thicken during the last few minutes of cooking and also as it cools in the saucepan or serving pot. So make it on the thin side.

* * *

The STOP ME AND BUY ONE ice-cream man on his tricycle cart in docklands and elsewhere, served blocks of ice-cream, wafers, cones, and water ice in a triangular stick that you pushed out of its container as you sucked or bit. I do not believe that anyone thought of adding sauce to the blocks made for home consumption. But there are lots of sauces for ice-cream that are available in the kitchen that are normally used for other purposes. They need no further preparation, or very little. So should you have dull ice-cream to use up, have a good look around the shelves and cupboards.

ICE-CREAM SAUCES

You will need:
Any of the following

A fine sauce is golden syrup, straight from its can or jar, or heated. When blended with melted butter it is even better.

Chocolate spread is another potential sauce. Jams and marmalade, straight from the jar or heated and diluted with a little water are other ideas.

Grated chocolate, cream, nuts, sultanas, currants, raisins and peanut butter, all make good sauces on their own or mixed.

Crumbled plain digestive biscuits may not strictly be a sauce, but it is delicious on ice-cream. But top of my list comes the hot chocolate sauce that follows.

* * *

I suppose that chocolate sauce, hot or cold, for ice-cream is one of the most popular of all. Fortunately it is simple to make. Here's how.

HOT CHOCOLATE SAUCE FOR ICE-CREAM

You will need:
Butter
Cocoa powder
Sugar
Vanilla essence

In a saucepan put a good lump of butter, and melt it. Add a spoonful or two of cocoa powder, about twice the total volume of plain white sugar, a drop or so of vanilla essence and a little water. Stir it into a paste over the heat and then add more water to make it just liquid. Stir or whisk all the time. Let it boil up to the rim of the pan once or twice. It will then be smooth and ready.

You can pour this hot sauce straight over ice-cream or put it into a jug to be served hot, and later, if there is any left over, cold. Make it in whatever quantity suits you.

Consider adding to it nuts and/or sultanas. Crumbled plain digestive biscuits, scattered on top of the sauce when served, creates an inviting look, texture and taste.

* * *

SOUPS

With the cooking range on the go for so much of the time in old dockland, soup was a natural, warming and economical way of filling hungry mouths. So there was often soup on the hob or trivet.

L eeks, because of their long season and reasonable cost, were always a favourite vegetable in dockland. This soup is not only simple to make but is one of the very best. I think it is just because the combination of leek and potato makes such an ideal marriage. The butter, and you should be generous with it, has also a bearing on the success of this "winner of soups".

LEEK AND POTATO SOUP

You will need:
Leeks
Potatoes
Butter
Salt and pepper
Water or stock

Take, say two or three
medium size leeks, cut
away and discard any rootlets,
rough outer skin and tatty
greenery. Now push a sharp
knife right through the centre
of a leek, fairly near to
its root end, and drag
the blade toward, and
right through, the green part.
Turn the leek on its side and do the same again.
You now have the solid white part near its root, and a split head of white and
green. Run the cold tap and with the tousled head pointing downwards under

the flow of water, rub and wash off any dirt that may be sticking to the "hair". Do this thoroughly, as a grain or two of grit in the soup can grate on the teeth and be unpleasant. Do the same with all the leeks. Then cut them up fairly finely.

Now peel and wash up to six medium size potatoes.

In a large saucepan, or pressure cooker to save time, put a large lump of butter. What is "large"? Well, it will depend on how much soup you intend to make. But with three leeks and six medium size potatoes, it could be a very generous dessertspoon full. Melt this slowly and into it throw the finely cut leeks. Stir them around in the melted butter.

Cut up the potatoes as finely or as coarsely as you like, and add these. Stir it all around. After a little time you will notice that the volume of your mixture has reduced a little. It is time to add some pepper and salt.

Now add as much water, stock (see the next recipe STOCK) or stock cube and water as desired.

Now it is just a case of boiling it slowly for an hour or so and then testing for saltiness. Thirty minutes in a pressure cooker is quite enough.

To add water is perfectly adequate, but to use stock instead of water will make the soup tastier. The kind and quantities of leeks, potatoes and butter will also make a difference.

Some soups (and other dishes, like stews) are often even better the next day. But if you are making soups to last over several days, bring them to the boil each day - especially if beans (pulses) form part of the ingredients. They are inclined to ferment.

* * *

Stock is simply water with more taste. Add it to soups, stews and gravies to make them taste better. Stock cubes add flavour. Oxo cubes, the favourite of dockland, will add colour as well as taste.

STOCK

You will need:
Water
Bones
Vegetables
Spices
Pepper and salt

If you boil spaghetti and retain the water from the pan, you will notice that this water has gained a little extra taste (and thickness). Use the same water to boil some carrots, and retain it. You will find it has acquired a little more taste, then Brussels sprouts - and so on. You are making stock, and not throwing away useful liquid.

But the best way to produce stock is from a boiled up mixture of bones, vegetables, herbs and spices. These bones, like meat or bacon bones, or the carcasses of boiled or roast chickens and ducks and suchlike should never be thrown away before all their tastes have been extracted by boiling them up in the stock pot. Some like to roast the bones first.

When I boil up bones I usually add a bay leaf, a small peeled onion, one clove of garlic, a stick of celery if there's one around, perhaps a clove or two, the smallest pinch of thyme and pepper and salt. Other vegetables can also go in - especially if you have a surplus or they look a little tired and limp. I also like to add a pig's trotter to the mixture. This gives taste and a gelatinous consistency to the stock. But not many people like to use trotters in the kitchen. Never add too much flavour in the form of herbs and spices. If you do, their tastes will dominate the stock. The art is to make a liquid that will enhance the flavour of whatever you are cooking.

Stock can boil slowly on the top of the stove in a saucepan with the lid on for almost as long as you care to let it, as was the case with the kitchen ranges of old dockland. Or much time will be saved if a pressure cooker is used, when boiling bones, vegetables and flavourings. Then 3/4 of an hour should be enough.

If you can't be bothered with all this palaver, make stock by crumbling a stock cube (meat, vegetable, fish or Oxo), or part of one, into hot water.

***

This is the most traditional of dockland soups. It is simplicity itself to make. But, like many a traditional dish when cooked on the range all day, it takes time. It is a robust, nutritious, filling, economical and tasty soup.

PEA AND BACON BONE SOUP

You will need:
Split peas (one packet)
Stock
Bacon bones or smoked
bacon
Pepper and salt
Mint
Then possibly:
Butter
Onions
Carrots
Turnips
Celery
Leeks

Soak the split peas overnight, changing the water often at the start and possibly adding a pinch of bicarbonate of soda.

Then you could simply boil the peas for a couple of hours or more with bacon bones or smoked bacon, pepper and salt, adding some mint before serving. Alternatively, with a good knob of butter cook chopped onion until transparent. Add the soaked peas, stock and bacon bones or bits of smoked bacon. Boil this slowly for about two hours or more, taking the scum off as it rises. Pepper and salt it. Or, about an hour before serving the soup, add grated or small pieces of carrot, turnip, celery, leeks, etc.

Add dried or freshly chopped mint before serving.

* * *

This fish soup is based on a white sauce (see page 49), like the traditional parsley sauce of dockland.

CREAM OF TUNA FISH SOUP

You will need:
Butter
Flour
Pepper and salt
Milk/water/stock
Dijon mustard
Cheese (grated)
Tuna fish from a can

Make your white sauce by melting a good lump of butter in a saucepan, adding flour to form a bubbly or dry paste, salting and peppering it and adding plenty of milk or milk and water or milk and stock before whisking it all together.

When the mixture begins to thicken, or even before, put in some Dijon mustard and a little grated cheese (like cheddar).

Now you have made the tasty white sauce, which can be thinned down to the consistency of soup by adding more milk, water or stock (fish if possible). Let it cook very slowly for a while and then taste it. You may feel like adding more pepper and salt.

Strain the contents of a can of tuna fish and, with your fingers, flake it into the soup. Stir and serve.

Cooked pasta is excellent when mixed into cream soups such as this one, giving body and texture. After boiling the pasta beforehand, save the water for the white sauce. Some added capers will stimulate taste buds. Incidentally, the soup will be even tastier the next day.

* * *

With the white sauce/soup mix you will be able to make many other cream soups. The list is endless.

OTHER CREAM SOUPS

You will need:
The white sauce/cream soup start
Other ingredients

Having made a saucepan full of basic cream soup, what might you add to give it distinction?

Try frozen peas for a pea soup, boiled carrot bits, asparagus pieces, chopped mushrooms, watercress, chopped hard boiled eggs, pasta, fish, chopped French beans, boiled and chopped onion, shellfish... Some items will need boiling before being added to the soup as otherwise they would be too hard. In these cases, always use the water to add to the soup, as that is where much of the taste lies, and nourishment, too.

Cream may be added to these soups at the last minute before serving. And a little chopped parsley sprinkled over the surface of the soup in its plate is always a winner.

* * *

This economical dish is a dockland/sailor's soup, the simple recipe coming from a rather strange Dutch cook (who was not popular in a Parisian brothel for misinterpreting the use of a bidet) on a coaster based at Dundee Wharf in Limehouse. Spent bones were thrown overboard in port or at sea.

CHICKEN SOUP

You will need:
Chicken leftovers, bones giblets etc.
Bay leaf
Stock
Pepper and salt
Onion
Butter
Turmeric
Rice

Boil or roast a large chicken and use the flesh as you will.

Boil the bones, carcass, skin and giblets in stock, or water with stock cubes, for an hour or two, adding pepper and salt and a bay leaf. Strain off the liquor and throw away the residue.

Fry a finely chopped onion in butter until transparent. Add the liquor to the onion. Make a paste of a level teaspoon of turmeric in water and add this. Throw in a handful of rice. Continue to boil the soup until the rice is very soft.

Should any chicken meat from the original roasting or boiling not be needed at the time, cut it up into small pieces and add them to the soup shortly before serving it.

If roasting a chicken with this soup in mind, coat the chicken well beforehand with a blend of thick, Greek yoghurt, 1/2 a teaspoon of turmeric powder and chopped fresh or dried tarragon leaves. The result of even roasting a tasteless, mass-produced bird, is a glowingly golden chicken with plenty of taste and style.

* * *

The following is a wonderful soup, but with a snag to it - or perhaps you might think it an amusing bonus. The fact is that this particular root vegetable, when cooked in almost any form, creates a great deal of air in the stomach and beyond. And as this air has to escape somewhere, and as a rule choosing to exit in the downward direction, it can cause embarrassment, laughter or pain.

ARTICHOKE SOUP

You will need:
Butter
Jerusalem artichokes
Onion
Potato
Pepper and salt
Stock or stock and milk

Melt a large lump of butter in a saucepan, and in it cook a chopped-up onion until it is soft. Add half a dozen or so well-scrubbed artichokes (they usually are knobbly and difficult to free of adhering soil) and a chopped potato. For a pale and finer soup, peel these vegetables. For a rustic one, don't bother. Season with pepper and salt. Cook for a little longer and add stock, or stock and milk, to cover generously. Boil this very gently for about half an hour. The vegetables will then be soft.

Now you have the choice of eating the soup as it is in its rough and ready form, liquidising it in an electric blender, or putting it all through a hand-operated food mill. I rather prefer the last method. Test for seasoning and serve.

* * *

Pumpkins, not mentioned to me as a dockland vegetable, are not just Halloween decorations for scaring away ghoulies and ghosties. They are for eating, too. Perhaps a bit bland on their own, they give body, colour and texture to many a winter dish. Here we concentrate on soup, but add the pink or yellow flesh (scooped out to make that toothy grin if you like) to stews, curries, casseroles, pig's trotters and whatever you fancy. Here is how to make the soup.

PUMPKIN SOUP

You will need:
Butter
Pumpkin
Potatoes
Onion
Carrots
Pepper and salt
Stock, or water and stock cube
Cream (optional)

Melt a good lump of butter in a saucepan and into it put chunks of pumpkin flesh and peeled potatoes in roughly equal quantities (but don't bother too much about the proportions). Stir them around. Now add a chopped onion and a few cleaned and chopped-up carrots. Add pepper and salt (remembering that if you choose to add a stock cube later it will be adding salt). Then cook the vegetables slowly for quite a few minutes.

Now add stock or stock cube and water to well cover. Cook for about half an hour until the vegetables are soft and then pass them through a food mill or liquidiser. The soup will then be ready. Pour a little cream into each serving if possible.

* * *

Watercress, with its peppery freshness and greenness, makes not only a crunchy garnish for many a dull-looking dish, but also a wonderful soup. Although watercress was a favourite in dockland, no-one has mentioned watercress soup. Here is how to make it.

WATERCRESS SOUP

You will need:
Watercress
Onion
Pepper and salt
Stock
Milk
Cornflour
Cream

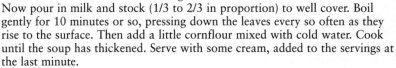

Well rinse, and cut up finely the stalks and leaves from one or two bunches of watercress. Dice a small amount of onion and, in melted butter, cook it with pepper and salt until the pieces become transparent. Add the watercress and cook for a little longer.

Now pour in milk and stock (1/3 to 2/3 in proportion) to well cover. Boil gently for 10 minutes or so, pressing down the leaves every so often as they rise to the surface. Then add a little cornflour mixed with cold water. Cook until the soup has thickened. Serve with some cream, added to the servings at the last minute.

If you do not like the soup in the roughish state, liquidise it or pass it through a food mill.

The soup may also be thickened with a little white sauce (page 49) instead of cornflour.

* * *

Dumplings are a joy to most people, especially in dockland of old. They are simplicity itself to make, economical, filling and nutritious. By adding them to a soup (or stew) you will enhance it and turn a modest dish into a meal. They are especially good in winter when soups and stews seem to be at their most welcome. Come in from cold blasts over land or river to a dish with dumplings and you will soon be warmed right through.

DUMPLINGS FOR SOUP (and stews)

You will need:
Flour (plain or self-raising)
Suet (that is, finely chopped or minced beef fat)
Salt
Herbal flavourings, possibly
Pease pudding, possibly

Make your dumplings in the same way as suet crust pastry (page 111) by combining twice the amount of flour by weight or volume to suet (like Atora). Include a little pease pudding if there is any at hand. Add some salt, stir together and then add water to form a stiff dough. Form this into balls, roughly the size of golf balls, and drop them into the just-boiling soup for 20 minutes to half an hour. They will then be ready to serve with the soup. If you use self-raising flour the dumplings will be fluffier. With plain, they will take up less space and be chewier.

So good are dumplings that there will almost certainly be calls for more. So it is a good idea to add some more to the soup (or stew) as soon as you have served the first helping. Then, in 20 minutes or so, there will be another lot ready to offer.

Plain dumplings are best, but many in continental Europe favour them mixed with herbs and spices. So here is an area in which to experiment. But start with plain ones.

* * *

PASTA

Pasta, except for vermicelli and macaroni, is comparatively new to dockland. Now it is a favourite food, especially for those new to the area. The first recipe is simple, and one of the most delicious ways of using the meat or tomato sauces already mentioned.

SPAGHETTI WITH MEAT SAUCE

You will need:
Dried spaghetti
Salt
oil
Meat sauce, or tomato sauce
for vegetarians
Possibly grated
cheese
Black pepper
from
a pepper mill

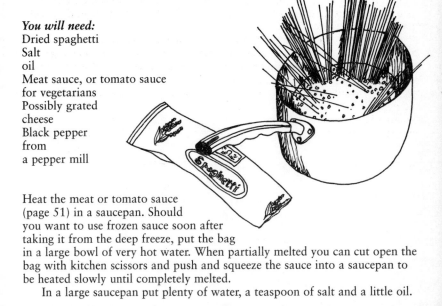

Heat the meat or tomato sauce (page 51) in a saucepan. Should you want to use frozen sauce soon after taking it from the deep freeze, put the bag in a large bowl of very hot water. When partially melted you can cut open the bag with kitchen scissors and push and squeeze the sauce into a saucepan to be heated slowly until completely melted.

In a large saucepan put plenty of water, a teaspoon of salt and a little oil.

Bring the water to the boil. Add dried spaghetti. Usually a packet would feed four very hungry people.

Put the spaghetti in to the boiling water and fan it out until it softens and sinks down into the water. Then give it a good stir. Some people break up the strands of dried spaghetti before cooking it. Purists like to cook it whole. Bring the water to the boil once more and rest the saucepan lid on top to keep in the heat but allow steam to escape. Turn down the heat until the water is just bubbling. In 12 minutes time the spaghetti will be ready (but always look on the packet to find the correct timings for that particular brand). Give it a stir after a few minutes from the start, to check on the bubbling and to once more separate the strands and prevent any pieces of spaghetti from sticking to the pan.

Strain the spaghetti in a colander and retain the water for stock if desired.

To slide the cooked spaghetti on to plates is a difficult task if not using spaghetti tongs. But you can use kitchen scissors to cut the pasta in the colander into the quantities desired. It is then quite easy to slide these on to plates. An Italian would hate that idea.

Add the hot or warm sauce to each plate, grind over some black pepper from a pepper mill, and serve.

Some people add grated Parmesan or other cheese to the spaghetti. This adds taste and richness to the dish, but is not essential.

Pasta comes in all shapes and sizes. Each shape can be used in the above way in place of spaghetti, but the thicker the dried pasta the longer it will take to boil. Again, look on the packet for details. Freshly made pasta may also be used. It will take a shorter time to cook but is not necessarily better to eat.

Italians like their pasta to be just firm enough to bite on (al dente) and not too soggy, like the canned variety. And if their ordered spaghetti comes to the table in under 12 minutes, short cuts will have been made in the kitchen and it will not have been cooked correctly.

***

The following is an absolute winner of a dish that I have served since dockland days to children and adults. However, it does take a little more time to cook than plain spaghetti and sauce, but it is well worth the extra effort, especially for a party. And it can be made well beforehand and stay bubbling in the oven for quite some time after it is ready for the table (always an advantage when guests may be late to arrive).

POP'S PASTA

You will need:
Meat sauce or tomato sauce (page 51)
Garlic
Olive oil
Salt and pepper
Pasta of any kind
Smoked bacon or slivers
of ham (optional but
very good)
Butter and plain flour
for a white sauce
Milk
Grated cheese
(like Cheddar)
Dijon mustard
Paprika (optional)

Find a large, open, ovenproof dish and over the bottom of it spread a quantity of basic meat or tomato sauce. Squeeze a garlic clove evenly over this. Do not overdo the garlic. Then dribble some olive oil over the meat sauce and garlic.

Now boil some pasta in salted water with a little oil until it is cooked (12 minutes for spaghetti and longer for thicker pasta). Cook more than you will need as you can make the start of a great soup with it and any sauce left over. Spread the pasta evenly over the meat or tomato sauce. Into it push slivers of bacon or ham if desired. This should almost fill the pot.

Now make a white sauce. Put a big lump of butter into a saucepan and melt it over low heat. Then add plain flour until the mixture is thick and bubbling. If you have added too much flour, don't worry. The mixture will be dry and crumbly. Now pour in cold milk or a mixture of milk and water (possibly spaghetti water). Put in, say roughly ten times the volume of the flour. Slowly cook this sauce until it thickens whisking it all the time to rid it of lumps. If it is too thin, cook for longer, if too thick, add more liquid.

You will need to add plenty of pepper and salt, as it seems to need more than you think. Now, when the sauce is the thickness of cream, add some grated cheese. The quantity is the amount you feel to be right, but, for a start, add, say, the gratings from a piece twice the size of the lump of butter. Too much will make the sauce greasy. Also add a heaped teaspoon of prepared Dijon mustard - two if you feel generous. Stir the sauce until the cheese has melted. It should be fairly runny and taste really good. The sauce might burn if the heat beneath it is too high. Avoid this by cooking it slowly and stirring constantly with the whisk. The whisk being rounded, and the corners at the bottom of the pan being sharply angled, sauce will hide all around the edges and tend to stick and burn. So as you whisk, use a spoon to stir this hiding sauce into the mixture. Cover the pasta with the white cheese sauce. Make sure that every bit of pasta and bacon or ham has been coated. A dusting of paprika over the top will make the dish look nicer. Heat it through in the oven.

Any sauce left over can have stock or water added to it for the start of a cream soup. Then put in any pasta left over. Turn this tasty and creamy start into a chicken soup, a green pea soup, asparagus soup, watercress soup, sweet corn soup, or any other kind of soup by adding a tender ingredient. Certain additional items might need to be boiled beforehand. Then adjust with salt and pepper if you think it necessary.

***

This is a dockland dish that grown-ups and children asked for regularly at a time when the word pasta was not in general usage, though macaroni meant pasta. It is a dish that has stood the test of time. I think that everyone, meat-eater or vegetarian, likes it. And an advantage of selecting this wholesome and easy-to-make dish is that it can be prepared well before needed at the table. So, if more convenient, it could be made at leisure, say in the morning, to be baked in the oven that evening.

MACARONI CHEESE

You will need:
Macaroni
A white sauce (page 49)
Dijon mustard
Cheese
Paprika

Buy dried macaroni, penne, rigatoni or spaghetti. In fact, you can use almost any kind of pasta, but the larger pieces, like penne or rigatoni, are the best for this dish.

Make a fairly liquid white sauce, adding a good dollop of Dijon mustard and grated cheddar cheese. As a rough guide, for a pint or so of the sauce try a heaped dessertspoon of the mustard and a tablespoon or two of cheese.

Boil the pasta until it is soft. For the penne size this will take about 15 minutes - less for smaller pieces. Stir the pasta every so often to prevent it sticking to the bottom of the pan. Strain it and possibly use the water to add to soup.

Spread the pasta evenly over the bottom of an ovenproof dish and cover it with the sauce, completely coating the pasta pieces. Sprinkle over some paprika - for looks. Bake the dish in the oven until the top is brown and the sauce bubbling.

Try to make more sauce than wanted. Add some pasta water to it and some leftover macaroni cheese from the dish. Judge it correctly and you will have made an excellent soup.

***

MAIN COURSES
VEGETABLES, FISH AND MEAT

*Main courses in old dockland were generally substantial, easy
to prepare and economical. It is a shame that many of the
traditional dishes have gone out of favour. They represent some
of the best in British cooking.*

Meat pudding was a regular item on the dockland family's menu. In many households it was eaten each week. And with the kitchen range on the go, to steam a pudding for two or three hours was not a problem. To use up any suet crust pastry that was left over when making the pudding, jam dumplings were made. So these two dishes often went together. I quote directly from a dockland source.

MEAT PUDDING
(and Jam Dumplings)

"Meat pudding was made with beef
suet and flour. You mixed the suet
and flour (half as much suet to flour)
with water into a dough then rolled it
out thin with a rolling pin. Line a big
white basin with the dough. Put the meat,
onion and Oxo gravy into the basin. Roll a
piece of dough out to cover the top of the
basin. Tie a piece of white cloth around the top
of the basin very tight. Heat some water in a saucepan, just enough to come
3/4 up the basin. Then it was put on top of the stove for 2 or 3 hours,
making sure enough water was still in the saucepan.

"The meat was usually leg of beef cut into small pieces. We had boiled
potatoes and peas with that.

"If there was any dough left over, my mum would roll it out into little
balls and drop them into boiling water for about 1/4 of an hour, take them
out, put jam on them. They were called jam dumplings."

***

Limestone from Caen, in Normandy, was transported by sea and river to be used extensively in the building of Westminster Abbey (1050-1056). The slabs were quarried from beneath the ground as malleable, soft, yellow/white stone. These hardened and became white during their sea voyage to England. They were offloaded at Thames-side wharves to be trimmed and carved by stonemasons to build and decorate the Abbey. These craftsmen came from all over Europe. There were Italian cathedral/abbey/monastery builders among them, and this was a favourite dish of theirs, involving plenty of garlic. To ensure a plentiful and constant supply, heads of garlic for flavouring, known since earliest times, would have been brought with them and the cloves planted in autumn for harvesting as full heads the following summer.

The dish was cooked at the same time as bricks were baked in ovens. So meat that needs long and slow cooking is essential to this most ancient of dockland dishes, one that scented the air around Westminster.

Black pepper, another essential ingredient, was known and used in Roman times. The tomato, however, did not appear in Europe until the early 16th century. So perhaps another vegetable was used, or none at all during this heyday of cathedral building between the mid 11th century until the latter part of the 13th century. Be that as it may, tomatoes are an essential part of this dish.

MEDIEVAL BEEF STEW

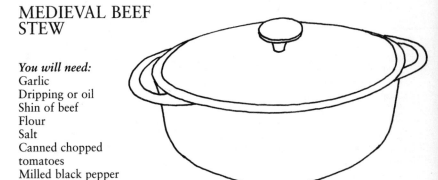

You will need:
Garlic
Dripping or oil
Shin of beef
Flour
Salt
Canned chopped tomatoes
Milled black pepper

Take an iron pot (with a close fitting lid) and put plenty of peeled cloves of garlic at the bottom of it. To be more rustic, you could use unpeeled cloves of garlic just as well, but diners will have to discard the coverings as they eat. Put in a little dripping or oil and add chunks of beef, cut from the shin of the forequarter. This meat is without fat and has a rounded, marbled look to it. Heat up the pot and turn the meat and garlic around until the meat has changed colour to brown. Add a dessert spoon of plain flour and turn this into the mix. Add salt. Now tip in the contents of a can or two of chopped tomatoes. The last thing you have to do is to mill over lots of black pepper. You may have to add some water, as the dish at the start should be on the liquid side.

Put on the tight fitting lid and bake in a slow oven for about three hours or on the top slowly for about two hours. Keep an eye on the liquid content as the dish is cooking and add water if necessary as you go. You might have to obtain the right consistency by taking off the lid and gently boiling away the excess liquid on the top of the stove. End with a thick gravy around the meat. I like to test the meat toward the end of the cooking to be sure that it is soft and not chewy.

This lovely and historical dockland stew could be made the day before it is wanted, or kept hot beyond the stage when the meat has been cooked. So it is a very useful, and somewhat festive, dish. Serve with mash or crusty bread.

***

Eggs and tomatoes go very well together, especially in a sandwich or in this creamy and delicious pie.

EGG AND TOMATO PIE

You will need:
Eggs
Tomatoes
White sauce (see page 49)
Mashed potato (optional)

Cut up tomatoes into slices and place them at the bottom of an ovenproof dish. Hard boil eggs (ten minutes from the point of boil, having put the eggs into a saucepan of cold water). Slice these thinly and place them on top of the tomatoes. Your eggs and tomatoes may now be used up, if not, start another layer.

Make a white sauce (page 49) and pour this over your sliced eggs and tomatoes. Give the pot a twist and shake so that the sauce permeates through the layers. Put a covering of mashed potato on top if desired. To do so will make the dish more substantial.

Bake the dish in a medium to hot oven until the sauce bubbles or the potato top becomes brown and crisp. Make sure it is well cooked and piping hot all through.

***

This is a classic dish in dockland and elsewhere that needs leftover or newly made mashed potato. If you are making the mash especially for this dish, make it drier than you would normally, adding less milk and only a little, if any, butter.

FISH CAKES

You will need:
Mashed potato
Cooked fish or canned fish, both without bones or skin
Pepper and salt
Parsley or corriander
Possibly flour, beaten egg and breadcrumbs
Oil
Onion, possibly

Put mash into a bowl, or keep it in the saucepan. Add flaked, cooked fish, smoked haddock, or the drained contents of a can of salmon or tuna fish. You might consider cooked mussels or other shellfish, possibly chopped.

Add chopped parsley and possibly more pepper and salt.

Do not mash up this mixture, but break up the lumps with a wooden spoon and stir the fish into the mash to form an even mix.

Now, with a little oil in a frying pan, you could cook the entire mixture as a large fish cake, turning it over in bits as best you can when the underside starts to become crisp. Alternatively, you could form the mixture into individual fish cakes, dipping them in seasoned flour and frying them on both sides.

And again, you might like a slightly more elaborate way of presenting the fish cakes by dipping top and bottom in plain flour, then in beaten egg and finally in toasted bread crumbs, before frying them to a crispness top and bottom.

Some fry onions first to be part of the fish cakes. But whichever way you do it, the result will be excellent. It will also be simple to make.

***

Stewed eels are among the great delicacies of dockland and probably best eaten in an eel and pie shop. But you may want to cook them at home. Then buy only live eels, getting the fishmonger to clean and cut them into small pieces. Use them right away.

EELS AND EEL PIE

You will need:
Freshly killed eels
Various bits
according to the
recipes below

STEWED EELS:
Wash the eel pieces in salted water. Just cover the morsels in water and cook very slowly for 30 minutes. Take them from the water and cover with a thin parsley sauce (page 49).

JELLIED EELS:
Cook the eels as above and add them to a little of the liquor in which you have dissolved gelatine. Allow them to cool by putting the bowl outside – in the days before refrigeration.

Another method is to add a bay leaf or two and a sprig of thyme to eel pieces packed upright and tightly in an ovenproof pot. Just cover with vinegar and bake slowly for two hours. Extract bay leaf and thyme and allow it to cool.

EEL PIE:
From the salted water as above, pack the eel pieces in a pie dish with stock and the juice of a lemon to cover. Cover the pie dish with short crust pastry (page 110) and bake in a hottish oven for about an hour.

Another recipe requires that you roll the eel pieces in pepper, salt and mace. Pack them into a pie dish tightly, cover with vinegar and bake them. Make a short crust pastry, cover the pie and complete the baking.

FRIED EELS (a favourite in Amsterdam dockland):
Take the pieces from the salted water, dry, and roll them in seasoned flour, and then possibly in beaten egg and toasted breadcrumbs (a tacky process). Fry them in oil or fat, or deep-fry until cooked and crisp. Deep fried parsley placed over all is delicious.

* * *

This dish needing mashed potato is one of the most popular if not the most popular in my household. Children and adults devour it with relish. A dockland edition is made slightly differently and may be eaten hot or cold. When cold, it is sliced like a cake and eaten with salad.

CORNED BEEF HASH AND CORNED BEEF PIE

You will need:
Mashed potato
Onions
A can of corned beef
Pepper and salt
Oil

Keep the mash in its saucepan or place it in a bowl. Chop up several onions fairly finely and fry them in oil until they start to brown and smell of fried onions. Put them with the mash. You might want to add a little more pepper and salt.

Open a can of corned beef. Be very careful when you do this, as when using the key supplied, the edges of the old-fashioned style can and its lid, when opened, are razor sharp. There is hardly a cook who has not been sliced by these sharp edges at one time or another. Consider using a can opener on the wider end of the corned beef can. The meat may not want to come out. Placing the metal in hot water to melt the outer layer will probably do the trick. If not, use the can opener to pierce a hole in the other end to allow air to enter and relieve the suction. Or even cut out this other end all together and push out the corned beef.

Having extracted the corned beef from its can, place it on the mash and onion and cut it into small pieces. With a wooden spoon stir these and the fried onion into the mash, breaking up any large lumps as you do so. Form an even blend.

Fry the corned beef hash (there should be enough oil or fat left over in the frying pan from cooking the onions). Turn the mixture over as best you can when the underside has become brown and crisp. Cook for a little longer.

The corned beef pie of dockland is made by putting a layer of moist mash in the bottom of a casserole, upon which is placed a layer of corned beef and herbs, then a layer of grated onion. These layers are repeated until reaching the top of the casserole. Complete with a layer of mash, which is coated by one of grated cheese.

Bake slowly in the oven for an hour or two.

* * *

Irish stew must be one of the best stews and almost certainly the most economical. However, whereas it is usually quite all right to add ingredients to recipes for Irish stew, you should keep to the basic lamb or mutton, onion, potatoes, salt and pepper and water. The Irish themselves are known to add carrots, and in dockland, pearl barley.

The meat you buy could be lamb, hogget, or older mutton. The cuts should be of the cheapest. Aim for scrag end and middle neck. Best end chops (coming next to middle neck) are more expensive, but excellent. The scrag end is the neck of the beast, with lots of bone, but the meat in and around it is very tasty and will add extra flavour to the stew.

An alternative is shoulder chops. They are good value for having more meat and less bone for a reasonable price. Bones and some fat are necessary ingredients for adding flavour to a good Irish stew. If the amount of fat seems too great (and it often is), do not cut it off the meat before making the stew, but make the stew well before it is wanted at the table (preferably the day before). If it is then left to cool for some time, or overnight, take off the fat, which will have solidified on the surface of the tasty liquid. Use a spoon or your fingers for this and either throw it away or add some to the dripping pot. Do not worry about the stew deteriorating if left overnight. On the contrary, it will taste even better when heated up a second or third time.

IRISH STEW

You will need:
Onions
Potatoes
Lamb or mutton
Pepper and salt

Cooking instructions are easy.
The quantities used are up to you.

Peel and cut up onions, enough to cover the bottom of a large, lidded saucepan. Cover these onions with a layer of peeled sliced potato. Now make a layer of the lamb or mutton bits. Add pepper and salt and pour in water to just cover the meat. Now complete the dish with a thick layer of sliced potato. The thickness of these slices is up to you, but be sure this last layer is a thick one.

Cook slowly with the lid on for about an hour or more, to be sure that the meat falls away from the bones. Take away the fat if desired, as instructed above.

Over each generous serving sprinkle a little chopped parsley if possible. Put a large plate on the table for bones.

* * *

Boiled salt beef has always been a favourite dockland dish. It was bought from street vendors, from the butcher, boiled or just pickled, and pickled and boiled in the home. Traditionally served with carrots, sometimes dumplings and often with pease pudding, it continues to be a popular treat.

Butchers are sometimes willing to pickle it on request. However, this process can easily be done at home.

When eaten in dockland with carrots, pease pudding and boiled potatoes, the liquor might then be used for boiling cabbage. The resultant liquid was served separately in cups as "green water".

Boiled salt pork was also popular, and often had pease pudding cooked with it at the same time.

BOILED SALT BEEF OR PORK

You will need:
Pickled beef or pork
Vegetables, such as carrots and potatoes
Pepper
Possibly dumplings (page 72)
Possibly pease pudding (page 35)

In a brine (see Glossary) pickle silverside, brisket or aitchbone of beef. Rinse the meat and put it in a pot and cover with water. Add a bay leaf and pepper (there should be enough salt from the brining). Bring to the boil, scumming it as anything rises. Lodge the lid of the pan over the pot to allow steam to escape and boil the meat for an hour. Now add your carrots, potatoes or other root vegetables and continue to boil until the vegetables are cooked.

If serving dumplings, put these in 20 minutes before everything is ready for the table.

If wanting green water, use some of the liquor to boil a cabbage.

Treat pickled pork in the same way.

This is not the normal dockland fish pie, when fish is cooked, boned, combined with a white sauce, covered with mashed potato and baked. It is one that is quicker and less trouble to prepare.

TUNA FISH PIE

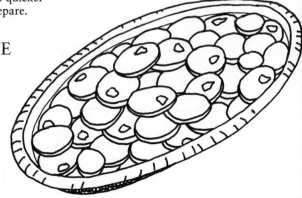

You will need:
Onion
Capers
Tuna from a can
Salt
Milled black pepper
Potato
Milk
Butter
Paprika (optional)

Grate an onion on to the bottom of an ovenproof dish. Take some capers from their brine and mix them with the onion so that the combination is evenly spread.

Open a can of tuna and pour away the oil or brine. Flake the fish into an even layer over the onion/caper mixture. Add salt and mill over some black pepper.

Peel potatoes and slice them thinly. Put a thick layer of these on top of the tuna. Make sure that the upper surface is level. Now pour in milk until it almost covers the potato, but not quite.

Cut butter into small pieces and place them all over the potato. Then, if you like, sprinkle a little paprika over all, for looks as much as anything.

Bake the dish in a medium to hot oven until the potatoes are cooked, the top is brown, and most of the milk has been absorbed by the potato or evaporated. It could take from 3/4 to an hour or more.

The dish, when ready, will keep hot and not spoil if left in the oven for some time after it is ready.

* * *

Keeping to the dockland theme of low cost, simplicity and nutrition, I include this dish at the request of an impecunious son who almost lives on it. The ingredients are easy to acquire. Moreover, it is quick to prepare.

TUNA AND BEANS

You will need:
Red beans in a can
Tuna fish in a can with its oil
Onion
Parsley (Optional)

Combine the beans, tuna in oil and chopped onion. Then eat. Decorate and present this dish for guests according to your artistic wiles, using chopped parsley as a garnish. You might like to substitute the tuna oil with vinaigrette. Dried red kidney beans are cheaper than those in a can. If bought in bulk and boiled in the quantities required, they can be used for this dish, chilli con carne, soups, etc.

* * *

To use any red kidney beans, possibly from the above dish, here is a recipe for what has become a favourite on the menus of dockland pubs.

CHILLI CON CARNE

You will need;
Dried red kidney beans (or those ready-cooked from a can)
Basic meat sauce (see page 51)
Oil
Chilli con carne powder (see page 122)
Salt

Obtain beans in a can or soak dried red kidney beans in a bowl of cold water for a day, night, or day and night. Cook them by boiling the beans in water vigorously for 10 minutes, and then slowly until they are soft enough to eat. The first 10 minutes is very important as during that time poisonous toxins will be boiled away. Allow 3/4 of an hour. But it could be more or less, depending upon the dryness of the beans.

Add chilli con carne powder and salt to a thawed-out packet of basic meat sauce. The amount of powder you add is entirely up to your taste, as are the proportions of beans to sauce. Then add the sauce to the cooked beans, pouring in some oil. Heat it all through, possibly adding a little water to get the consistency of the sauce to your liking. Then this filling, tasty and economical dish is ready for the table. Any left over will be fine to eat the next day, or can be added to soup.

* * *

Shepherds, who handle sheep, traditionally use minced lamb or mutton to make shepherd's pie. Cottagers may use beef in the same way to make cottage pie. Whoever the cook, and whatever the meat or methods used, the following recipe makes a splendid pie, and one that may be offered to shepherd, cottager, landowner or docklander alike.

COTTAGE AND SHEPHERD'S PIE WITH A VEGETARIAN ALTERNATIVE

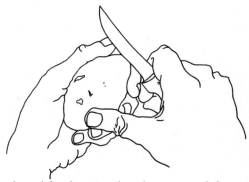

You will need:
Mashed potato
Minced lamb, mutton or beef
Onions
Oil or dripping
Pepper and salt
Worcestershire sauce
Tomato ketchup
Gravy browning (optional)
Cornflour (possibly)

Cut up a lot of onions fairly finely and fry them in oil or dripping until the pieces become brown and the smell mouth-wateringly good. Add the minced meat, breaking up any lumps as it cooks through (a potato masher is good for this). Pepper and salt it well and shake in some Worcestershire sauce and tomato ketchup. I then add a little gravy browning for looks, but this is not necessary. Now add water to just cover and cook the mixture slowly until the liquid has become a thickish gravy. Should you have added too much water, the mixture may be thickened, when the mince is thoroughly cooked, by the addition of some cornflour mixed with a little cold water. Taste the pie filling. It may need adjusting by the addition of a little of this or that. The addition of some basic meat sauce (page 51) is excellent. When it tastes really good, put the mixture into one or several ovenproof pie dishes. Cover the mince with a good layer of mashed potato, made without much butter or milk. Roughen up the top surface with the tines of a fork and bake the pie in a medium oven until it is thoroughly heated through and the upper surface golden brown.

For vegetarians, substitute cooked and chopped mixed vegetables for the minced meat. Use carrots, leeks, parsnips, swede, turnip or greens. Otherwise proceed exactly as described above.

NOTE: Tomato ketchup will provide both sugar and vinegar to the sauce. So you might also consider adding either or both of these when 'adjusting'.

* * *

Stews were the regular standbys of wives in dockland. They were sustaining, economical, easy to keep hot on the hob over a long period of time, and were much appreciated by tired dockers and children at the end of the day. The lamb, beef and rabbit stew recipes come directly from a lady in dockland.

LAMB STEW, BEEF STEW, SAUSAGE STEW, RABBIT STEW, AND SAUSAGE AND SMOKED BACON STEW

For the lamb and beef stews you will need:
Lamb or beef (cheap cuts)
Pot herbs (see Glossary)
Pearl barley
Gravy with Oxo cubes

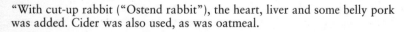

"Into a pot put the cut-up lamb meat, vegetables, pearl barley and gravy with water, in total up to 2/3ds full. Cook slowly for 2-3 hours.

"Beef stew was cooked in exactly the same way with dumplings added 20 minutes before dishing up.

"With cut-up rabbit ("Ostend rabbit"), the heart, liver and some belly pork was added. Cider was also used, as was oatmeal.

"Sausage stew was made in exactly the same way as the other stews but did not need to be cooked for so long."

The following sausage and bacon stew was popular among the Irish in dockland.

For it you will need:
Sausages
Smoked bacon
Pepper and salt
A herb of your choice
Onions
Potatoes
Parsley if you have any

Cut up sausages (of any variety or mixture) and smoked bacon into small pieces or strips. Put them in a saucepan with pepper, salt and a herb of your choice (thyme and sage are good). Just cover with stock or water, boil for 5 to 10 minutes and drain off the liquid into a bowl. Depending on the fat content of the sausages and bacon a certain amount of oil will rest on the surface. Those who are against eating too much animal fat will take this off with a spoon and discard it.

Now cover the bottom of a lidded casserole with peeled, chopped onion. On it put a layer of peeled and sliced potatoes. On this place the sausage and bacon mixture, followed by another layer of chopped onion and a thick layer of sliced potatoes. Now add the liquid produced by boiling the sausage and bacon bits.

Ignore the level of liquid in the pot, as your addition of the initial cooking liquid and that made as the stew cooks should be enough.

Put on the lid, which should be tight fitting. Bring to the boil on top of the stove and cook slowly for about 3/4 of an hour - until the potatoes on the top are soft and the dish smells appetising. You may then continue with very gentle cooking for another hour or so if you are not ready to eat right away. If you are using floury potatoes and are worried about the liquid level, check it. Serve with some chopped parsley on each plateful.

If you do not finish the dish at one sitting, it will be fine the next day and the day after. But check the liquid level content before you reheat it.

***

This is a recipe that is very easy to make if using minced meat or Basic Meat Sauce (page 51). A favourite in dockland without the curry powder, and a favourite of Indians with it, this is a good, cheap and filling dish.

CURRIED MINCE AND PEAS

You will need:
Minced beef or lamb
Basic Meat Sauce (page 51)
Curry powder
Pepper and salt
Fat or oil
Peas (frozen or fresh)

Put the mince in a saucepan with some fat or oil, adding curry powder, pepper and salt. Cook it well until it is brown and there are no longer any lumps. Or if using basic meat sauce, add curry powder to taste, salt and pepper. Heat it up. Now add peas (all quantities are up to you). Add a little water. Stir. Bring the mixture to the slow simmer until the peas are cooked. Check on the moisture level during the cooking and add more water if necessary. Also check that there is enough salt.

***

Trotters were a favourite in dockland and eaten hot or cold with bread and margarine. They were simply boiled. Foreigners introduced more exotic ways of cooking them. I include one of these, and refer to cow heel and sheep's trotters.

PIG'S TROTTERS

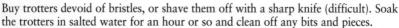

You will need:
Trotters, split or whole
Pepper and salt
Bay leaf and other herbs and spices of your choice
Vinaigrette

Buy trotters devoid of bristles, or shave them off with a sharp knife (difficult). Soak the trotters in salted water for an hour or so and clean off any bits and pieces.

Boil them in water into which you have added pepper and salt, herbs and spices. Boil until the meat falls from the bones. For this allow up to 2 hours, or 45 minutes in a pressure cooker. Serve the trotters alone, hot, warm or cold. Vinaigrette goes well with trotters, and if to be served cold, turn them in vinaigrette when still hot or warm. Keep them moist thereafter.

Trotters may also be boned, the gluey meat cut into small pieces, and served in a white parsley sauce. This is also the best way of serving sheep's trotters, or feet. But boil them for 2 1/2 hours before boning and serving with the sauce.

This is a Mediterranean method of cooking trotters - also cow heel pieces. If using cow heel, substitute the words cow heel for trotters.

For this you will need:
Trotters (or cow heel, cut into small pieces)
Pepper and salt
Celery
Onions
Beans, dried or canned
Chilli
Garlic
Tomato paste
Cumin

Treat the trotters as above and boil them for 1 1/2 hours with celery and onions.

Boil beans that have been soaked overnight (red kidney beans are good), for ¾ of an hour without salt. Or take them straight from a can.

Fry onions until browning, adding salt and a chopped and de-seeded chilli. Add some crushed garlic and tomato paste, cumin, and enough water to make a thin sauce. Cook the sauce until it thickens and add the cooked beans, trotters and vegetables with some of the liquor. Simmer for a further 1 to 1 1/2 hours, until all the ingredients have amalgamated happily, possibly adding more liquor if they seem to be drying out.

Use the liquor in which the trotters have been boiled as stock for soups and stews.

All the less popular parts of an animal were enjoyed (or tolerated) in lean times by those who lived in dockland. A pig's head, or half of one, with all its parts, from ear to chap, was as much prized as any. It provided a variety of excellent dishes and at a reasonable cost. As a student I could entertain and feast off a pig's head for at least a week. So I have a great affection for the following recipes.

PIG'S HEAD

You will need:
A pig's head or half of one
Salt and pepper
Butter, vinegar and capers for the brains
Flavouring of vegetables, herbs and spices for the boiling
Flour, egg, breadcrumbs and garlic for the ears
Sharp gravy for the tongue
Gherkins, herbs, onion, etc. for the brawn

Having selected a pig's head that has been well de-bristled, get the butcher to divide it for you (keeping the tongue intact) and ask him to remove the eyes. Extract the brain and cover this for a short time with boiling salted water. Remove the outer membrane. Fry slices in butter, to which you have added a little vinegar and a few capers. Serve as a dish on its own.

Cut off the ears. Wash them and the head thoroughly and put them in well-salted water for 12 hours or overnight. Then boil the head, ears and tongue in a large pot with salt and pepper, bay leaves, peppercorns, and token flavourings of garlic, onion, carrots, celery and the like. After 2 to 2 1/2 hours the meat will start to fall off the bone. Lift out the head and ears, and when cool take all the meat off the bone. Throw away the bones and teeth. They, and the eyes, are of no use. Strain the liquor, saving most for other uses and a little to reduce for the brawn. Use the liquid for soup, stews or stock. There will be quite a lot, so perhaps freeze it in bags if you have the space and facilities.

Take the ears, which have a certain crunchiness to them, and cut them into slices, which you then dip in flour, beaten egg and breadcrumbs. Fry the strips and serve them with garlicky mayonnaise. Being head meat, like some sausages with too much of it in them, they will tend to stick to the pan.

Skin the tongue, slice and serve with sharp gravy (page 59).

The jaw meat pieces on either side are the Bath chaps. Separate these from the rest and press them into a mould or basin. When cold, heat the outside of their container and extract them. Coat with toasted breadcrumbs. Slice and serve with pickles.

The rest of the meat will become a substantial brawn. Into a bread tin or bowl or pot of your choice, lay strips of the cold head meat interspersed with sliced gherkins, green peppercorns, chopped onion, garlic, capers, lots of chopped parsley and any other items, spices or herbs of your choice. Press it all down.

Now reduce some of the retained liquor and add some gelatine to it. Pour this over the meat and flavourings, shake it in so that it permeates right through into cracks and crevices, and on top put a board and a heavy weight. Juice may overflow. So do this on the sink's draining board. Allow the brawn to cool. Either extract it from the container by heating the outside as above, or leave it in its pot. Slice the brawn across the line of strips and serve with mash, pickles, or in sandwiches with plenty of mustard.

Is it any wonder that in times of dockland poverty, such a modestly priced item, one that could be turned into a varied collection of healthy and substantial dishes, was so prized.

* * *

A lady recalls that in her dockland youth the sight of a huge platter of vegetables with a sheep's head sitting in the middle put her off eating meat on the bone ever after. I am sure that many people would be in sympathy with that opinion. It is true that some strength of stomach is needed to tackle and eat a sheep's head. But there are people who love it. A calf's head looks rather friendlier. I eat it in France with pleasure, but would not enjoy cooking it. For those who do not mind, this is what to do.

SHEEP'S HEAD AND CALF'S HEAD

You will need:
Sheep's head or calf's head
Vegetables, like carrots, turnips, onions and celery
Bay leaf and thyme tied together
Pepper and salt
Butter, vinegar and capers for the brain
Rice or pearl barley

SHEEP'S HEAD
Remove the brains if the head has been halved and extract the tongue. Soak the brain in salted water, slightly boil it, take away the membrane, slice, and fry quickly in butter to which you have added a touch of vinegar and a few capers.

Take the head and tongue and soak them in salted water overnight. Discard the water. Cover again with salted water. Bring this to the boil and discard the water. Now cover once more with lightly salted water and boil slowly for 3 hours, skimming at first to remove any scum that rises. Then add vegetables, a small handful of pearl barley or rice, and cook until these are ready. Put the head, tongue, vegetables and some of the liquor on to a large platter. Cut off the meat and serve with the vegetables.

CALF'S HEAD

Treat a calf's head in just the same way as a sheep's head, but boil it for 2 1/2 hours. Cook it with or without the vegetables. If without, serve sliced with a parsley vinaigrette.

* * *

Calf's foot and cow heel were popular in dockland because of their economy. Like pig's trotters, both contain more meat than expected. And the liquor is excellent as stock for soups and stews.

CALF'S FOOT AND COW HEEL

You will need:
Calf's foot or cow heel
Salt and pepper
Bay leaf and thyme
White sauce, possibly
Vegetables, possibly
Parsley sauce, possibly
Sago or tapioca, possibly

CALF'S FOOT

Having soaked a calf's foot overnight in salted water, bring it to the boil and discard the water. Boil it again, this time for three hours in lightly salted water with bay leaf and thyme. Cut away the meat, discarding bone. Having cut the meat into small pieces, serve it in a white sauce (page 49) into which you have added plenty of chopped parsley. The foot may also be boiled with vegetables. The recipe is for one foot, but two or more would be better.

COW HEEL

Get the butcher to cut up the heel into several pieces with a band saw. Treat them in the same way as calf's foot.

An alternative to white parsley sauce is to add a tablespoon of sago or tapioca to the meat and liquor. Then boil it for a further 25 minutes.

Cow heel may also be cooked in the same manner as the trotter and bean recipe on page 92.

* * *

Cabbage has always been a dockland favourite vegetable, but it has mostly been plain boiled. Now there are many more imaginative ways of cooking it. The following recipe uses cabbage as a vehicle for cooking sausage, belly of pork, tough game birds and much else. The humble cabbage then becomes part of a truly wonderful dish.

CABBAGE, POTATOES, SAUSAGE, ETC.

You will need:
Green cabbage, like January King
Olive oil
White wine or cider
Potatoes
Pepper and salt
Sausage, hocks, belly
of pork, trotters,
game birds, bacon,
etc.

Cut a firm green
cabbage into
quarters and then cut
out all the hard core
inside. Now cut the cored
quarters into small pieces
and put them into a heavy casserole. On the cabbage pour a good slosh of olive oil and just a little liquid in the form of white wine or cider. Add pepper and salt. Now stir it all around with a spoon or with your hands until the cabbage pieces glisten.

You may think that there will not be enough liquid in the pot, but cabbage is mostly water and you will have added some more.

Now put some peeled whole or halved potatoes on the cabbage.

For vegetarians you have done enough. For carnivores it is time to put on top of the cabbage some well-pierced sausage, preferably of the Polish boiling ring variety, belly of pork or any of the other items mentioned, and perhaps some not mentioned. Surround the meat with the potatoes. Put on the lid, and place the casserole in a medium to hot oven for about 2 hours, or perhaps 3. The lovely smell in the kitchen will indicate about when the dish is ready. But it will keep hot in the oven quite happily well beyond the time when it is ready.

Then eat it. But leave some goodies in the pot for the start of a wonderful soup by cutting what remains into small pieces and adding stock.

***

Liver and bacon was a favourite dockland dish. The following recipe comes directly from a Limehouser.

LIVER AND BACON

You will need:
Lamb's liver sliced
Bacon
Lard
Flour
Gravy (Oxo) or stock
Potatoes
Greens or peas

"Wash the liver slices and dip them in flour. Melt lard on a frying pan and put in the liver. Add bacon at the same time. Take out the liver and bacon when ready and add flour to the residue in the pan. Cook for a little longer and add gravy or stock to make thick gravy.

"Serve the liver and bacon with potatoes or boiled greens or peas. Cover with the gravy."

* * *

Pancakes were eaten on Shrove Tuesday in dockland. Otherwise they did not feature much on the daily menu. The following recipe is a very popular one with children, can be made fairly quickly, and is ideal to serve with drinks if guests are coming for a short visit.

THICK CHEESE PANCAKE

You will need:
Oil
Garlic (optional)
Self-raising flour
Eggs
Dijon mustard
Salt
Milk
Cheddar cheese

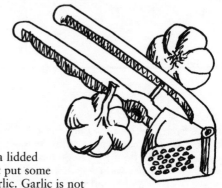

Coat the bottom and sides of a lidded frying pan with oil, and into it put some finely chopped or squeezed garlic. Garlic is not absolutely essential for this dish, but almost.

Into a bowl sieve a quantity of self-raising flour (say 1lb.). Make a crater in it and into this break two eggs. Add a dessert spoon of Dijon mustard and some salt. Use a whisk to break up the eggs and stir them around, adding half a pint of milk or more as you stir outwards. When the milk has been incorporated and the batter neither thick nor thin, beat it to eliminate all the lumps. This can all be done in a blender if you like. Now add grated cheddar cheese - say a small handful. Too much will make the pancake greasy.

Heat the oil and, when the garlic is just turning brown, add the pancake mix to form an even covering of the pan. On medium heat, and with the lid on, cook the pancake until the edges are drying, bubbles appear on the drying upper surface and the pancake no longer sticks to the pan (a good shake will tell you when it is free). Then toss it, or turn it over. Make cuts in the newly exposed upper surface for moisture to escape, leaving the lid off until the pancake has been cooked.

Ease the golden pancake on to a wooden board, for preference, and cut it up, or allow your friends to cut off pieces for themselves.

You will probably find that this dish is so good that in future you will make more batter and start a second pancake as soon as you begin to eat the first.

* * *

Faggots were a favourite dish in dockland. But because such items as minced lungs, windpipe and spleen are added to liver, hearts and anything that was handy for the mixture, cooking the dish was usually left to the butcher. Bought hot or cold, straight from the baking tin or individually wrapped in caul fat, they were eaten with pease pudding. Some then turned bought faggots into a home-made faggot stew. To make your own faggots, the following recipe is more or less how you would go about it.

FAGGOTS AND FAGGOT STEW

You will need:
Minced pork or lamb
Some or all of minced liver, hearts, lungs, windpipe and spleen
Fat
Breadcrumbs or rusk
Spices
Herbs, like parsley, sage or thyme
Salt and pepper

Mix your choice of the above ingredients in any proportion thought appropriate. Dampen with water or stock if necessary. Put it all into a greased, shallow baking pan and bake in a low oven for about two hours, until the top becomes crusty.

FAGGOT STEW
Put plenty of potatoes and onions in a saucepan without much water and no salt. When cooked, strain off most of the water and place faggots on top. Continue to cook slowly until the faggots have been heated through. Then mash it all together.

* * *

This is a regular dish in dockland households. It is one of the few dishes that I make, keeping to certain rules and measurements. This is only because I failed so many times before a Yorkshireman (who could cook Yorkshire pudding and nothing else) told me the secret. Now I seldom fail.

The final and delicious result is usually eaten with roast beef, but is also eaten on its own covered with gravy (page 58) or consumed as a dessert coated with jam, syrup and such. It can be reheated, or eaten cold with butter and jam, etc. When cooked with currants it becomes Black Jack.

YORKSHIRE PUDDING (BATTER PUDDING) AND BLACK JACK

You will need:
Plain flour
Salt
Eggs
Milk
Dripping or some other oil or fat
Currants for Black Jack

Into a bowl sieve 7 heaped dessert spoons of plain flour. Make a crater in the middle and into it break two eggs. Add salt. Make up 1/2 pint of 2/3 water and 1/3 milk.

Break up the eggs with a whisk and, working outwards from the centre, add the milk/water mixture slowly as you stir, until all the liquid has been added and a batter formed. Beat this until there are no longer any lumps to be seen in it. This is done with most success well before it is wanted for the oven. Then it is whisked again several times. The more whisking before going into the oven, the better it will be. However, the Yorkshireman in question made his successful puddings immediately before putting them into the oven, only whisking once.

The batter is now ready to add to a scalloped or large baking pan in which a good coating of dripping, oil or fat has been heated to a high temperature in the oven. When the batter is poured into the hot pan it should rise and curl at the edges. Now quickly put the pan into the very hot oven for 20-30 minutes.

For Black Jack, cook the Yorkshire pudding with lots of currants added to the batter.

* * *

This 'favourite' dish is made in exactly the same way as Yorkshire pudding (page 100), except that sausages are heated in the dripping or oil before being surrounded by batter.

TOAD-IN-THE-HOLE

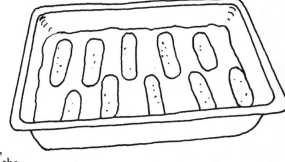

You will need:
Yorkshire pudding
batter (see above)
Sausages

Make the Yorkshire
pudding batter as
directed on page 100,
and when heating up the
dripping, oil or other fat, brown the sausages all over. Now, when the
dripping is very hot, surround the sausages with batter, making sure that the
sausages are evenly spaced in the baking tin. Cook in exactly the same way as
Yorkshire pudding.

* * *

Ox-tail was a popular winter dish in dockland. It was also an ideal dish
for cooking in or on the kitchen range, needing to be cooked over a long
period of time. Cooking differed a bit from the "throw it all in" type of stews
as a little more preparation was needed.

OX-TAIL

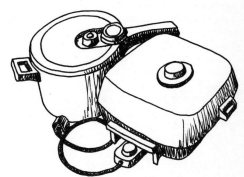

You will need:
Lean ox-tail
Flour
Pepper and salt
Dripping, butter or oil
Onion
Gravy or stock
Gravy browning
Vinegar

Select lean pieces of ox-tail from the butcher. There is no point in buying too
much fat if it is to be discarded later. Soak the pieces in salted water, dry, and
coat them with well-seasoned flour. Heat dripping, oil or butter (butter makes
the dish richer) in a heavy pot and brown them. Take them out. In the

remaining fat, fry cut-up onion until it turns brown and smells of fried onion. Return the ox-tail pieces to the pot and add any seasoned flour left over from the coating process. Stir. Cover with gravy (Oxo) or stock to which you have added a little gravy browning, for looks, and a dash of vinegar. Put on the lid and cook on the top of the stove or in the oven (best) very slowly for 2-3 hours or longer. Occasionally check that the dish is just bubbling and not drying out. The meat should come away completely from the bone.

Serve with mash to absorb the delicious juices, or with potatoes baked in the oven at the same time as the ox-tail.

* * *

Tripe and onions has been a popular dish in dockland for years, though there is little demand for it nowadays. Some butchers supply bleached tripe in the winter months to the few who still eat a dish that, to me, seems like eating rather chewy rubber. But then it is an animal's stomach, so I suppose it must be on the firm side. I have ordered it in restaurants in Normandy, where it is made in the Caen way, and still wished I had chosen something else, even though I love trotters and calf's head, etc. However, here is how to cook it in both the dockland and French way.

TRIPE AND ONIONS

You will need
Bleached honeycomb tripe
Onions
White sauce (page 49)

The dockland method:
Cut the tripe into small squares and simmer them in stock with onions until soft (a long time). Make a white sauce, using the stock. Combine the tripe, onions and white sauce.

The French method:
Soak cut-up, cow heel and honeycomb tripe in salted water for several hours. Cut the tripe into small squares and put them and the heel pieces into a pot with salt and pepper, onions, carrots, bay leaf and thyme. Cover with cider into which you have added a good slug of brandy or calvados. Cover and cook in a moderate oven for 10 hours. Remove and discard the vegetables, fat and bones before serving the tripe very hot in an earthenware container.

* * *

SWEETS

The main course followed by a sweet was the meal of old dockland. The sweets were as important as the main course, and appreciated just as much. That some were fattening was unimportant.

This coffee cake was always a children's favourite and required no cooking. And it is very easy for children to make. It stores well if put into a tin in a cool place.

HEDGEHOG COFFEE CAKE

You will need:
Margarine or butter
Caster sugar
Broken biscuits or plain
digestive biscuits
Coffee essence (Camp Coffee)
Almonds
Currants or peppercorns

Put a fairly large lump of margarine or butter into a bowl and place this in a warm spot for the fat to soften. Now cover the margarine or butter with twice its volume of caster sugar. Mix with a wooden spoon until the two are blended well together.

In another bowl crush together enough broken biscuits (available in times past), or plain digestive biscuits, with your fists and fingers until you have about twice the volume of the butter/sugar mixture. Add the finely crushed biscuit to the butter/sugar mix and work it all together with your hands. Now add a little coffee essence, say a teaspoon or two to test for taste. Work this in.

The result will be crumbly and just sticky enough for you to roll it into a rough ball. Put this on to a plate and form it into the shape of a hedgehog.

Into the body stick flaked almonds to form spines. Then add currants or black peppercorns to make two eyes and a nose.

Now place the hedgehog in the larder or refrigerator to set.

At first make a small hedgehog, as it is very filling.

* * *

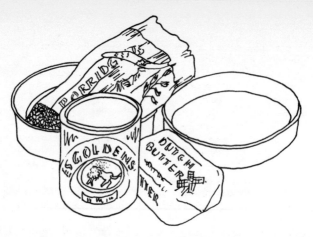

This dockland favourite with adults and children has the huge advantage of being very easy to make. Besides that, the result is irresistible to eat, and can be consumed at any time at all - at breakfast time, mid-morning, lunchtime, tea time, supper and when about to go to bed.

FLAPJACKS

You will need:
Butter or margarine
Golden syrup
Porridge oats

Put a large lump of butter or margarine (say 1/4 of a pound) into a bowl. Open a tin of golden syrup and put it and the bowl containing the butter or margarine into the oven on a low setting. Keep an eye on them and retrieve when the butter has melted and the syrup has become easy to pour. Add about three times the amount of syrup to the volume of butter or margarine. Stir them together. Now slowly add the raw porridge oats until you have obtained a dryish and slightly sticky mass. You are now ready to cook it.

Take a shallow pan, or several, and grease their inner surfaces by rubbing butter or margarine all over until the entire surface is coated. Now tip in the sticky mass, or some of it, and pat it down with a wetted spoon until the mixture is about as thick as your thumb. Now bake the tin or tins in a medium oven until the sides of the mixture are beginning to turn a brownish colour. It will not matter at all if you keep opening the oven to have a look. They are now ready to take out and to be cut into squares with a wetted knife. Allow the mass to cool and when cold take them from their tin, or tins, and break the pieces apart with your hands. Put the flapjacks into a lidded biscuit tin for when wanted. They are so good they won't last long.

***

Ice-creams were popular in dockland of old and will continue to be so everywhere. Although the lovely custard ice of the past has gone, to be replaced by ones made of other than milk and cream. They can still be made with pure and wholesome ingredients at home.

Machines for making ice-cream vary from the old-fashioned bucket of salted ice containing a drum in which the mixture was placed, to the simple frozen drum. The old way involved a long and laborious handle-turning to make an ice-cream that sometimes tasted salty. A very popular vendor of ice-cream in East India Dock Road added a great deal of salt to his. And so popular was this salty ice-cream that there was generally a queue of people outside his shop waiting to buy it.

At the other end of the mechanical scale are the stainless steel machines where the liquid is poured in and an electrical switch turned on. But the cheapest, if not the easiest, is the frozen drum method. A double skinned metal drum is placed in the freezing compartment or deep freeze for a day or two until it is really cold. Taken out and encased in a plastic outer drum, the blades are positioned, the liquid ingredients added, a lid put on and a handle added. With a complete rotation of the stirring blades accomplished every so often, ice-cream is formed to be eaten right away when ready, or put into a container to be frozen. When mine are frozen thus, they need about half an hour or so to soften up before being served. Some mixtures take longer.

ICE-CREAM OF VARIOUS KINDS

You will need:
Sweetened condensed milk
Single or double cream
Fruit pulp etc.

Using the frozen drum method described above, make your mixture from a can of sweetened condensed milk with single or double cream. To it add fruit that you have put through the hand operated food mill. That's it. But here are some tips: Before you freeze the drum, fill it with water and see how high this comes in your mixing basin. That mark will be the maximum height for the combined ingredients. Put the condensed milk into the basin first, then the fruit pulp, then the single cream, stir and cool right down in the refrigerator before you start to make the ice cream.

Strawberries can be added straight from the food mill. Raspberries, blackberries and gooseberries need to have their pips strained out before being added, with blackberries and gooseberries sieved after being cooked with sugar and a little water. Biscuits (digestive best) need to be crumbled first. Mango is best bought in a can as pulp. Apples need to be cooked down in a little water with skins, pips and all before being sieved and cooled for the mixture. Oranges and lemons need only to be squeezed and free of pips. Lemon may need extra sugar. For chocolate you will need to first make a thick and smooth mixture of sugar, cocoa powder and water. And for the rest? It is worth experimenting.

***

This is a dockland favourite food if ever there was one. All of those to whom I have spoken on the subject glowed with enthusiasm at the very thought of bread pudding. Hot or cold, if mother made it or if the baker made it, eaten before school, after school, for dinner, tea or supper, this was what life was about in "the olden days" or when down "Memory Lane".

BREAD PUDDING

You will need:
Stale bread
Eggs
Sugar
Mixed spice
Dried fruit (sultanas, currants, etc.) or
Mixed fruit (dried fruit with peel of
various kinds)
Margarine or butter

All measurements are at you whim, your degree of affluence, or feel for proportion.

In one bowl put stale bread in lumps or in thick or thin slices. Cover them with water.

In another bowl put dried fruit or mixed fruit, extra peel possibly, mixed spice, beaten egg(s), a little flour, sugar and a lump of margarine or butter. The more mixed fruit and peel, the richer will be the pudding – until it can almost be Christmas cake.

Now squeeze out the water from the bread and add the damp result to the aforementioned ingredients. Stir the pudding, or put your clean hands in and work it all together. Have a baking tin or other oven-proof container cleaned and greased at the ready.

Put the mixture into the greased baking tin and cook the bread pudding in a low oven for some 2 hours or more. Cover the tin for a soggy pudding or uncover for a drier one with a crisp top. Eat hot or cold.

***

Although I have mentioned in the Thick Cheese Pancake recipe that pancakes were eaten in dockland mainly on Shrove Tuesday each year, pancakes are winners for both children and adults alike, at any time of the year. They are simple to make, and most versatile. So they fit in well with dockland food. Make them to eat hot with any filling of your choice, or cook and keep or freeze them for when wanted later, possibly with a filling and covering of sauce. Strangely enough, although easy to make, when you start it might seem difficult. But after the first attempt, and getting to know how to make the batter, discovering the correct heat needed, and how your frying pan takes to it, cooking them will be easy from then on.

THIN PANCAKES

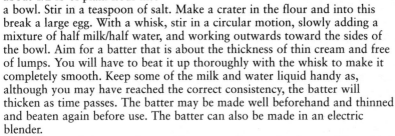

You will need:
Plain flour
Salt
Egg
Milk
Butter

Start by using one frying pan. Later, you will be able, if you are very quick and nimble, to have two going at the same time.

Make your mix by sieving about 1/2 lb of plain flour into a bowl. Stir in a teaspoon of salt. Make a crater in the flour and into this break a large egg. With a whisk, stir in a circular motion, slowly adding a mixture of half milk/half water, and working outwards toward the sides of the bowl. Aim for a batter that is about the thickness of thin cream and free of lumps. You will have to beat it up thoroughly with the whisk to make it completely smooth. Keep some of the milk and water liquid handy as, although you may have reached the correct consistency, the batter will thicken as time passes. The batter may be made well beforehand and thinned and beaten again before use. The batter can also be made in an electric blender.

Heat your frying pan thoroughly on a medium to hot burner. Dip a thick wodge of folded kitchen paper into soft butter and quickly rub the butter around the pan to completely cover the bottom of it, being very careful not to burn your fingers. Tip a tablespoon of batter into the pan (you will soon find the right size spoon for the frying pan) and then twist and turn the pan around so that just a very thin layer of batter coats the bottom of it. Put the pan back over the heat.

When the edges of the pancake start to shrink and just turn brown, turn the pancake over with a spatula. The other side will soon cook. Serve the pancake right away or keep it, with those that follow, in a low oven or beneath a low grill until wanted. Start another right away. Practise makes perfect. Warning. The first pancake of the batch will probably stick to the pan and be a failure (but good to eat). So butter the pan well at the start. Be sure there is nothing still sticking to the bottom of the pan when you butter it for the next one. From now on, a light but complete coating of butter will do.

Carry on cooking until hungry mouths are filled or catered for. Any pancakes left over, or those made when using up surplus batter, will keep well if bagged up when cold, sealed, and deep frozen.

Some popular coatings and fillings are lemon juice and sugar, jam or honey, syrup, maple syrup, each with or without butter. Grated cheese, bacon, sausages, crisps, fish fingers, baked beans, and chocolate chips or spread, are some of the others. Distribute the filling evenly over the surface, or place whatever filling you choose in the middle of the pancake, roll it up and eat with the fingers.

For a main course, these pancakes may be filled with a cooked stuffing, such as curry, sausage meat, bacon and scrambled egg, chicken in a sauce, mince and peas, fish or vegetables, etc. Roll the filling into the pancake and place it, with others, in an ovenproof dish. Cover with a white cheese sauce (page 50), possibly sprinkle a little paprika over the top for colour, and bake in the oven until they are well heated through and the surface is bubbling.

***

Cakes were exceedingly popular in docklands, and much looked forward to by the children. I give the three following recipes exactly as I received them from a lady in dockland who was born soon after the turn of the 20th century. I have added rough measurements.

LARGE FRUIT CAKE, SEED(Y) CAKE, COCONUT CAKE

You will need:
Flour (1/2 lb.)
Sugar (1/2 lb.)
Butter (1/4 lb.)
Margarine (1/4 lb.)
Eggs (2)
Milk
Currants (1/4 lb.)
Sultanas (1/4 lb.)
Candy peel (1/2 lb.)

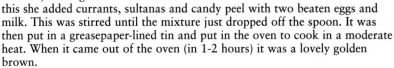

"Our Mum made a large fruit cake. In a mixing bowl she rubbed flour, sugar, butter and margarine into a fine mixture, looking like breadcrumbs. To this she added currants, sultanas and candy peel with two beaten eggs and milk. This was stirred until the mixture just dropped off the spoon. It was then put in a greasepaper-lined tin and put in the oven to cook in a moderate heat. When it came out of the oven (in 1-2 hours) it was a lovely golden brown.

"Seedy cake was made in the same way using caraway seeds instead of fruit.

"Large coconut cake was made in the same way as fruit cake. Instead of fruit, desiccated coconut was used." (Another lady I spoke to used only unlaid eggs for her coconut cake – unlaid eggs with soft or no shells being taken from the bodies of dead hens when killed for the pot.)

***

Some people, in dockland and elsewhere, seem to be able to make wonderful pastry, and with great ease, others struggle. Some have secrets and theories, others just go ahead and hope for the best. With both sweet and savoury fillings, making pies and pastry with reasonable results is easy.

There are two main kinds of pastry - short crust and suet crust. The former is for pies and open tarts and the latter mainly for steamed puddings and dumplings. For both kinds you will need half the weight of fats to flour. Once you have gained that vital piece of information you will more or less know how to make pastry. Here, in more detail, is how you go about it. Or buy it ready-made.

SHORT CRUST PASTRY

You will need:
Flour
Fat(s)
Salt
Egg
Sugar for a sweet pie

Into a basin put, say, about 4 oz. of butter, lard, or combination of both, and 8 oz. of sieved plain flour (note that there is twice the amount of flour to fat). Put in a teaspoon of salt and, if it is to be a sweet pie, a tablespoon of caster sugar. Cut it all together with a knife, and then rub it in the finger tips, letting the blend fall back into the bowl from above, to form a mix that looks like breadcrumbs. Some use a machine for the whole process. Then add a beaten egg or an egg yolk. Stir this in with a wooden spoon. After, if needed, bit by bit, add a little cold water to form a stiffish dough. A trick with many (some say it is essential) is now to put this dough, wrapped in greaseproof paper or foil, into the refrigerator for half an hour. Purists insist on everything being ice cold - even the hands. (You see how the secrets and mystery can multiply.) Roll out the dough on a smooth, floured surface with a floured rolling pin, never turning the pastry over. Certain cooks favour marble as the surface - cold marble, obviously!

Grease your baking tin with butter or lard and line it with a sheet of pastry (the thickness is up to you). Cut away the surplus from around the edges and blend these bits in with the remainder to be rolled out again for the pie lid if it is to be that kind of pie (except for when making a really rustic pie (page 113). Some now bake the unfilled pie case (open flans especially) for a while to dry it, so that the ingredients will not make the pastry soggy. But the lining may shrink or fall inwards - prevented by filling the case with rice, dry beans, or even small stones in greaseproof paper.

Fill the pie with cooked meat and gravy, cooked vegetables, or, if a sweet pie, fresh fruits with sugar, jam, syrup and beadcrumbs, mincemeat, etc.

A pie funnel or upturned egg-cup may be needed for the centre of a deep pie to separate the pastry lid from the filling.

Dampen the edges of the filled pie with water (use a soft brush) and cover it with a lid of pastry. Cut away the surplus pastry that hangs over the sides. Press together the lid and the lining. Pierce the lid to let steam escape and paint over milk or beaten egg to give the pie a nice colour when it has been cooked. Bake in a medium to hot oven until the pie looks and smells good enough to eat - about 1/2 an hour, usually.

Pastry like this is fine for simply covering a pie dish filled with cooked steak and kidney in gravy, or other filling. It may also be used for a Cornish pasty when a circle of pastry is cut, half of it covered with a cooked meat/onion/carrot/potato mixture, folded over and sealed down on itself when the joining edges have been well dampened with water. Pierce the pasty to let out the steam when it is cooking. Jam is another filling. Cornish miners, who needed substantial and simple fare to eat in their hands, took a double pie to work, half meat and half sweet.

***

Having just dealt with short crust pastry, we now get on to the much simpler suet crust pastry. This is used mainly for steamed puddings (page 114) and dumplings (page 72).

SUET CRUST PASTRY

You will need:
Flour (plain with baking powder, or self-raising)
Suet
Salt

Keeping to the principle above of half fats to flour, this time use minced suet (like Atora), to sieved flour. Mix in some salt and baking powder if not using self-raising flour. Add water and stir with a spoon, or mix with your fingers, to make a ball of thickish dough. Roll it out, as above, with a floured roller on a floured board.

***

I can do no better than give you the following recipes just as I heard them in dockland.

APPLE TART, MINCE TART, JAM TART AND TURNOVERS

You will need:
Flour
Margarine
Lard
Cloves
Apples
Sugar
Jam
Mincemeat

APPLE TARTS
"The tarts were made on a large dinner plate. The dough was flour, margarine and lard, made by putting these ingredients into a mixing bowl and rubbed together until it looked like fine breadcrumbs. This was mixed with water to make a dough, put on to a pastry board and with a rolling pin rolled out thin. The greased plate was lined with it and in it placed sliced apple and sugar with just a little water for juice. A few cloves could be put in for a nice flavour. Then another piece of pastry was rolled out to cover the apple and a couple of holes pricked in the pastry. When the pie was cooked, it was sprinkled with sugar."

JAM TARTS
"Made in the same way as the apple tarts but with jam and no cloves."

MINCE TARTS
"These were also made in the same way as apple tarts, but with mincemeat."

TURNOVERS
"Any dough left over from making these tarts was made into turnovers. These were circles of dough into half of which went filling. The edges of the dough were dampened, folded over and sealed. They were also pierced before baking.

"Small tarts were made in a tin with 12 little tins in them."

* * *

This apple pie can look pretty ordinary, but it is very easy to make and, with the added taste of pips and skins boiled together, will taste as good as any. What makes it rustic is that the pastry is laid in the pie dish, filled and the surplus pastry hanging over the sides folded over the top. Hey presto. No finesse. Nothing fancy. Dead easy.

RUSTIC APPLE PIE

You will need:
Short crust pastry (page 110)
Cooking apples (like Bramleys)
White and brown sugar
Butter or lard to
grease the tin

Peel and core your apples.
Put the peel, core, pips and
tough bits into a saucepan
with brown sugar and some
water. Boil it gently for some
time, but be sure it does not
dry out and burn. In another
saucepan put the white apple
flesh with plenty of white sugar and
a little water. Boil this until the apple
becomes a pulp.

Having rolled out your pastry until you have a disc somewhat larger than the greased pie dish or tin, lift the pastry over the greased dish and press down on it to make it fit the bottom and sides. Some will hang over the edge. How much does not matter.

Fill the pie with the amount of pulp you have made, and over this sieve the sticky brown juice from the boiling-up of skins and pips. Use a wooden spoon to help press as much of this as possible through the sieve. Be very careful doing this as the syrup will be very hot. Fold the hanging-over pastry inwards. That's it, except for baking the pie for about half an hour in a medium to hot oven. It will be ready when the pie smells good and looks brown on top. Eat it hot or cold, at home or outside with picnic food.

Of course, this pie can be made in a less rustic manner by trimming off the surplus pastry, rolling it out again, cutting it into strips, laying or interweaving these over the pulp in your desired patterns and then pouring the dark syrup over the top of it all. Cook as above.

* * *

Steamed puddings are one of Britain's and dockland's oldest dishes. In times past they were made to be substantial and filling. It is the same today. They are dishes for winter, when the cold winds blow over town, dock and river, and when appetites are great. They are festive, too, and surprisingly, easy to make, if a little time-consuming to cook. A bit fattening? So what!

STEAMED PUDDINGS–
Steak and Kidney, Sausage and Onion,
Vegetable, Treacle Pudding,
Spotted Dog, Spotted Dick
and Jam Roly-Poly.
(See also Meat Pudding on
page 78 for Jam
Dumplings.)

You will need:
Suet crust pastry (page 111)
Savoury meat, or sweet fillings

Line a greased, lidded basin (one made for steamed puddings with a clip-on lid) or a collared basin, with a rolled-out coating made from about half of your suet crust pastry. Fill it with, say, cooked steak and kidney in gravy, or sausage and onion in gravy, cooked vegetables in a sauce or, if a sweet one, golden syrup, breadcrumbs and grated lemon peel for a treacle pudding, marmalade, jam, stewed fruit or a filling of your imaginative choice. Dampen the edges to be joined and put on your pastry lid. A useful tip in forming this lid is to start by upending your basin on the rolled out dough and, with a little to spare, cut around it. Put this aside until wanted for the top of the pudding. Then, after lining the basin and trimming away surplus pastry, you may have bits of dough left over to cut up and add to the more liquid fillings, such as jam, syrup and such, that would otherwise make the dish too runny. These bits can be stuck to the sides as you fill the pastry lining by wetting and attaching as you go. Put on the dough lid.

Now for the steaming: Clip on the pudding lid or, with a pleated piece of greaseproof paper, tie it down with an elastic band or string. The old, traditional, method is to cover the filled basin with a square of clean cloth, made of cotton or linen, tying it beneath the lip of the basin collar with string, then tying the four corners in a knot above. This forms a convenient handle, and the cloth may be used time and time again. It looks nice, too.

In an inch or two of water in a saucepan, rest the basin on an upturned saucer or a perforated trivet made for the purpose. Saucers tend to jump about a bit. Add water to about half way up the basin. Cover the saucepan, bring the water to the boil and, keeping to the 'just boiling' point, cook for 2-3 or more hours - checking the water level every so often to make sure that it has not boiled away. When the level gets too low, add boiling water to raise it.

When the meat puddings were cooked for many hours on the kitchen ranges of dockland past, there was no need to pre-cook the ingredients. Your pudding will be wonderful to eat, served straight from the bowl or turned out on to a dish.

I now quote from an original source concerning boiled sweet suet puddings in dockland past:

"A boiled suet pudding was called a spotted dog, a roly-poly or spotted dick. It was made with flour, suet, mixed fruit, sultanas and raisins. When it was all stirred together, water was added to form a dough. Then it was rolled into a sausage-like shape, put into a flowered cloth, tied at each end, put into boiling water and put on the fire hob to cook for a couple of hours. Sometimes the dough was made into a round shape and tied at the top.

"A jam roly-poly was made the same way as the fruity suet pudding, only the mixture was just suet and flour. When it was taken out of the cloth, you cut a slice and put jam or syrup over it, or just sugar."

Others consider that a jam roly-poly should have the jam spread on to the dough, rolled, and edges dampened and sealed, before being tied in a floured cloth and boiled.

* * *

Junket was a popular dish between the wars in dockland. It is now generally out of favour.

JUNKET

You will need:
Milk
Sugar
Rennet
Nutmeg

Warm the milk to the heat at which it might have come from the cow and pour it into a serving bowl. Add a teaspoon of sugar, and rennet to the amount stated on its container. Stir and allow the junket to coagulate in a warm place in its bowl or in mugs for about 2 hours. Dust with grated nutmeg.

* * *

Rice pudding, tapioca pudding and sago were school foods and not always accepted with delight by the young, yet they were popular in dockland. Rice pudding was certainly a regular dish and ideally suited to the cooking facilities of the time. Tapioca and sago have almost disappeared from shop shelves. The rice and tapioca pudding recipes are directly from dockland.

RICE PUDDING, TAPIOCA PUDDING, SEMOLINA AND SAGO

You will need:
Rice
Milk
Sugar
Margarine or butter
Nutmeg
Tapioca
Semolina
Sago

RICE PUDDING

"Put the rice in a dish and cover with cold water. Let it stand for a while to swell. Then strain. Put the rice back into the dish and cover well with milk and sugar. Add a little knob of marg, stir well and grate nutmeg all over the top. Put it on the bottom shelf of the oven to cook slowly. The nutmeg gave a brown top to the pudding."

TAPIOCA

"Tapioca was made in exactly the same way as rice pudding."

SEMOLINA

Boil a pint of milk and on it sprinkle 2 oz. of semolina. Add some butter and stir and boil until the semolina is clear. Add a pinch of salt, 1 oz. of sugar and flavouring, like vanilla or nutmeg. Turn into a greased pie dish in which you have placed some jam, golden syrup or black treacle. Bake for 30-40 minutes in a moderate oven.

SAGO

Put 2 tablespoons of washed sago into a buttered pie dish with sugar, butter and milk. Grate some nutmeg over all. Leave it to stand for an hour. Stir well and place in a hot oven for up to 1 1/2 hours.

* * *

Blancmange was always a favourite with dockland children. Some parents would make pink, or double coloured ones – white and chocolate, pink and white, etc. This needed the mixtures made in two separate bowls and one colour poured into the mould before the other.

BLANCMANGE

You will need:
Cornflour
Caster sugar
Milk
Bay leaf or vanilla
Cocoa or artificial colouring (red for pink)
Jam

Mix 2 oz. of cornflour and 2 oz. of sugar with a little milk from a pint. Boil the rest with a bay leaf and allow the leaf to steep in the milk for about a quarter of an hour. Extract the bay leaf. Or add vanilla essence. Combine all and boil for 3 minutes until thick.

Rinse the inside of a mould with cold water and into it pour the mixture. Allow the blancmange to set. Serve with diluted jam.

For parti-coloured blancmange, divide the mixture, colouring one or the other with artificial colouring or cocoa made into a paste. Pour them into the mould separately.

***

ODDS AND ENDS

THAT DO NOT FIT IN ELSEWHERE

Bread and dripping was, and is, a dockland staple, though some prefer toast and dripping. It gives wonderful flavour to roast potatoes when they have been boiled previously for 10 minutes and coated with melted dripping, then peppered and salted. It adds flavour to numerous other dishes when used instead of other fats or oils. But not any old fat goes to make good dripping. Primarily it should be beef dripping. So roasts of beef are either covered with fat or beef fat added to be rendered down as the roasting takes place. Lard is another excellent addition, as is the fat from a duck or goose. Sheep's fat should be added sparingly.

DRIPPING

You will need:
An oven-proof dripping pot
Melted fat from roasts

When roasting, and having recovered the melted drippings, add them to the dripping pot and put this back into the oven when it has been turned off. Refrigerate the pot when cold, and whenever about to make a stew, a dark soup or gravy, cut out the fat which will have risen to the top and extract the lovely jelly which will have settled on the bottom. This dark jelly is far tastier and better than stock cubes or other flavourings. So even if the idea of dripping is abhorrent to you because of the dreaded word "fat", keep a pot going just for the jelly.

When eating it as bread and dripping or dripping toast, sprinkle salt on to the dripping and mill over some black pepper. If you are able to mix in some jelly with the dripping, so much the better.

* * *

Olives are new to docklands, as is olive oil. Certainly until some time after WW2 olive oil was only obtainable from the chemist, I think to be warmed and put into the ears to dissolve wax. Now both olives and olive oil are commonplace. The following is a good way to store olives.

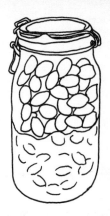

MARINATED OLIVES

You will need:
Olives
Olive oil

In a snap-down topped jar put black and/or green olives of your choice, but not without stones. These have been emasculated and lost much of their taste. Add olive oil to the jar, say to 1/4 up from the bottom. Turn the jar upside down every so often. This will keep the olives moist in oil. Top up the olives and the oil when necessary. As time passes, the oil will become darker and tastier, flavouring the olives. Tip them into a handsome bowl to serve. Return those not eaten to the jar.

***

Porridge was a breakfast *must* in many a dockland household. The oats were also used in soups and stews. Moreover, they provided a hot, cheap and substantial start to many a child's or adult's day. This is the method of making it given to me from a lady in Limehouse.

PORRIDGE

You will need:
Oatmeal
Salt

The proportions are roughly 1 measure of oatmeal to 2 1/2 measures of water.

"Boil 3/4 of a saucepan full of water to which you have added a teaspoon of salt. While the water continues to boil, add coarse oatmeal very slowly while stirring. When the porridge begins to thicken, stop adding the oatmeal and start stirring vigorously."

***

The Irish in dockland made soda bread, but otherwise bread making was mainly left to the baker.

Bread making is surrounded by mystique. Much fuss is made about a complicated process that can be simplified so easily. To follow the normal procedure of dough making, knocking down, kneading and all the rest, is rather time and energy consuming, if not tedious - though satisfactory. There is no need to do all this if you follow these simple instructions. The resultant loaves will be firmer and more satisfying than the bought variety. Children generally prefer the bought variety, which is better for sandwiches and making breadcrumbs.

MAKING BREAD

You will need:
Bread flour, brown or white
Dried yeast
Bran (optional)
Rye flour (optional)
Honey or other sweetener
Porridge oats
Butter or other fat or oil for
greasing the tins
Sesame seeds (optional)
Whole, soft wheat grains (possibly)

For a 1.5 kg. packet of strong bread flour (brown or white) have three standard bread tins at the ready (I bake six at a time to fill my oven). Prepare these by rubbing butter, fat or oil around the insides, coating the surface completely. Do not bother if you leave a lump or two of butter sticking to the sides or bottom. Pour in some porridge oats and turn the tins around so that the grains stick to the butter. Do this over a bowl to catch any oats that fall. Place the tins in a warm place. I have discovered that resting them on two wooden shelves above a lidded electric frying pan half filled with simmering hot water is ideal. Above a hot boiler is another good place.

Empty the 1.5 kg. packet of flour into a large bowl and to it add a tablespoon of salt, a tablespoon of dried yeast, a heaped tablespoon of rye flour (optional) and a tablespoon or two of bran (again, optional). Add any oats left over from coating the tins. Stir the dry ingredients together.

Put a little honey, sugar, syrup or other natural sweetener in a jug that will hold three pints. Add very hot water (from a tap if you like) and stir until the honey has dissolved. Now add this liquid to the flour mixture, stirring all the time with a wooden spoon. The result, when the three pints (or just more or less) have been added, will be a tacky mass. Depending on the brand of flour used, you might need just a little more water - but only a very little. The final amount of water added is very critical. So be cautious.

Divide the tacky mass equally between the three bread tins and leave them near to a heat source. This can even be in the sunny corner of a warm room.

Do not worry if the surface of the doughy mixture is rough or the tins unevenly filled. Do not cover them. Sprinkle over some sesame seeds if you like.

The bread mixture will take up the shape of the tins and rise in the warmth. It could take 2-3 hours or more - or less. As soon as the tins look a bit like tins of bread and have not yet overflowed, place them very gently in an oven that has reached a very high heat. Bake at this high heat for 1/2 an hour, and then for another 1/2 an hour at a low to medium heat.

Take the tins from the oven and tip out the loaves on to a wire rack to cool. Then eat and/or bag them for the freezer. They freeze wonderfully. If you do not consume a great deal of bread, halve the loaves before freezing them. And to keep the bread fresh over a period of time, wrap, and place it in the refrigerator.

Start with this simple recipe, with or without the rye flour and bran. Later, you may feel like experimenting by adding currants, nuts, caraway seeds, softened wheat, sesame seeds (plain or toasted), marzipan, candied peel or anything else.

I now add whole wheat to my simple bread mix. For this be sure to buy the soft, rounded wheat and not hard, pointed durum wheat. Allow 1/2 lb. per 3 loaves and soak the grain for 24 hours beforehand, changing the water every so often.

* * *

When making pastry (see pages 110 and 111) you may well have some left over. It is a very good idea to turn this into cheese straws, to be cooked in the oven at the same time as a pie, tart or whatever. The straws may be eaten hot right away, or stored in a lidded tin when cold, to be eaten later.

CHEESE STRAWS

You will need:
Leftover pastry
Cheese
Dijon mustard

Put your leftover pieces of pastry in a bowl and add some grated cheese (of almost any kind that will melt) and some Dijon mustard. Work it together with a spoon or with your hands to form a savoury kind of pastry. Form it into a ball. Then, as before, on a floury surface with a floured rolling pin, roll it into a shape roughly to fit a baking tin or tray. Grease the tin or tray and in it lay your pastry. Now, with a sharp knife, score the pastry (almost through) in parallel lines. Bake this in the oven until the pastry is golden brown. Extract it and allow it to cool. Then break the strips into cheese straws.

* * *

Chilli con carne has become a favourite item on the menus of dockland pubs. Many people will make it at home, as it is cheap, filling, nutritious, and winter warming. In fact, it is a true dockland dish.

I am always surprised at the cost of chilli powder mixture when the rest of the various ingredients for making a chilli con carne are so cheap to obtain. So should this powder be part of your kitchen armoury, you might like to make up your own brand. Buy the ingredients from an Indian grocery store, where they generally have plenty of spices for sale in larger quantities and at much cheaper prices than elsewhere.

MAKING CHILLI CON CARNE POWDER

You will need:
Cumin powder - 1 measure
Chilli powder - 1 or more measures
Paprika - 3 measures
Powdered garlic - 1 measure
Oregano - 2 measures
Salt - 1 measure

Mix them together and store in an airtight jar. See page 88 for the chilli con carne recipe.

***

A GLOSSARY

A

AITCHBONE — the hip, or rump bone joint of a cow or ox, popular in dockland at Christmas time or when the money was good and there were lots of mouths to feed.

ANDREWS LIVER SALTS — very popular, sparkle-producing powder in a tin, used for hangovers, indigestion, etc.

ANTIMACASSAR — generally crocheted material used as drapery or placed on the backs of chairs and settees to prevent men's hair oil from spoiling them.

ARROWROOT BISCUITS — hard white biscuits made from the rhizomes of a West Indian plant.

ARBROATH SMOKIES — closed, small, fine-fleshed haddock, hot smoked.

ASPIDISTRA — a popular house plant in dockland with long, tough, evergreen leaves.

B

BAR SOAP — cut from a long bar and weighed by the shop-keeper. Red or yellow, it was used for clothes, scrubbing floors, faces and bodies. Later it was sold unwrapped in three squares with the brand name printed on it. Later still, it was wrapped, with two cakes to a packet.

BEECHAM'S PILLS — rough, yellow laxative pills in a round box. Sold as being "worth a guinea a box".

BILE BEANS — black, bitter, laxative pills.

BILLET SOAP — the name used by the manufacturer for long bars of household soap sold under a brand name and cut for the customer as required. See bar soap.

BISTO — a popular gravy mix for flavouring, thickening and browning.

BLACKLEAD — graphite for blacking kitchen ranges or door-knockers.

BLACK JACK — a batter pudding with lots of currants.

BLACK PUDDING — a sausage containing pig's blood and some or all of the following — onions, fat, boiled pearl barley, breadcrumbs, oatmeal, cream, fresh herbs, salt, mixed spice and sugar.

BLANCMANGE — a pink or multicoloured cornflour dessert, set in a mould.

BLOATERS — a closed, salted and cured herring with roe inside.

BLOCK SOAP — also bar soap, scrubbing soap and billet soap.

BLOCK SALT — a solid block of salt from which table salt was scraped or grated into a jar or salt cellar. Or it was cut into lumps for pickling, salting down runner beans and such.

BLUE OR BLUEING — a small bag containing blue colour for laundry, to make whites appear whiter.

BLUE POKE — half pound packets of sugar wrapped in blue paper (sugar paper).

BRINE — a liquid salt mixture to preserve and colour meat (see Salt Beef or Pork). A mixture might be 3 quarts of water, 2 oz. saltpetre, sometimes 2 lb. of brown sugar, 2 lb. granulated salt and 1 oz. of bicarbonate of soda. This mixture should be boiled, a bag of herbs and spices added and then allowed to cool. The meat is then put in and kept in the cold brine from 3 — 10 days. To immerse floating meat, a scrubbed board can be placed on top and weighed down with a flat clean stone (like the kind found on a beach). The bag of spices could contain juniper berries, mace, sage, garlic, a piece of nutmeg, thyme, peppercorns and cloves. Butchers now generally buy pre-prepared ingredients for their brine.

BROWN SAUCE — bought sauce in a bottle, like Brand's, Daddie's, A1, HP and OK. etc.

BUBBLE (bubble and squeak) — mashed potato mixed with greens and fried.

BUNGALOW BATH — a name for a human-size zinc bath.

C

CARBOLIC SOAP — a soap containing the antiseptic/disinfectant carbolic acid, or phenol. The most famous was the red Lifebuoy soap, changed within the last few years to white and without the carbolic element. However, made in South Africa, the red is still available from Indian shops in a mild carbolic form. For real, strong carbolic soap, Carib Carbolic is available, also from Indian shops.

CARBOSIL SOAP POWDER — a carbolic soap for washing clothes.

CAT'S MEAT MAN — vendor of meat unfit for human consumption, sometimes selling the meat threaded on to sticks.

CAUL — lace-like white fat, peritoneum, sometimes used to cover faggots.

CHAPS (Bath chaps) — the cheeks of a pig's head, boiled, pressed and breadcrumbed, sometimes around a bone.

COLLEGE PUDDING — steamed pudding with dried fruit and spices.

COPPER — a large copper water container, heated from below by any combustible material available. Also a penny.

CROCHET — open needlework, contrived with a hooked needle.

D

DABS — small brown flatfish.

DAMPER — a metal plate in a stove flue with which to control draught.

DC —Direct current.

DEW SLUG — a small snail.

DOCKER — a man who loads and unloads ships.

DRIPPING — the substance produced by heating fat, usually beef fat.

DUBBIN — a greasy preparation for preserving and waterproofing leather.

E

EDWARD'S SOUP GRANULES — a popular soup mix at 2d a packet.

EXLAX — a chocolate laxative.

F

FAGGOTS — rissole-shaped small squares of minced meat and herbs, formed in a baking tin or individually wrapped in caul fat. Usually consisting of pork or lamb, fat, breadcrumbs, spices, parsley, sage or thyme, usually containing the pluck (liver, hearts, lights and windpipe) or spleen. Cooked very slowly and eaten hot from the oven, fried, deep fried or cold, generally served with pease pudding. Kept for some time beneath a layer of lard, before the days of refrigeration, it was a great favourite in Docklands but has now almost disappeared — with the demise of the local butcher. But where butchers do remain, some will make faggots in the wintertime.

FAIRY SOAP — a green soap sold in tablet form.

FIREBOX — where burning coal or coke is retained in a kitchen range.

FLICKERS — A series of stiff cards pinned together to give a moving picture when flicked.

FLUE — a pipe ducting smoke and fumes away from a stove.

G

GREEN WATER — when salt beef and carrots had been cooked, cabbage might then be boiled in the liquor. The result was green water, and this was served in cups with the salt beef, carrots and cabbage.

H

HOB — the top of a cooking range with removable circular iron plates.

HOGGET — see mutton.

HUDSON'S SOAP POWDER — the powder generally used for clothes washing, especially in the copper, though sometimes used for washing children's hair. It was bought in strong paper packets, round and 7"-8" high.

I

INDIAN TOFFEE — candy floss, but brown.

ISINGLASS — a gelatin made from the bladders of fresh water fish, but generally meaning water glass (sodium silicate in water) for preserving eggs.

J

JOYSTICK — a long cigarette costing 1½d, cut to size and much favoured by schoolboys who would light up and smoke them behind the bike sheds during a break, and continue with the same cigarette during further breaks.

JUNKET — milk curdled with rennet.

K

KIPPERS — split, cold smoked herrings, now usually dyed and flavoured.

KNUCKLEBONES — a popular dockland game for children, related to jacks.

L

LASCAR — a sailor from the East Indies, dressed accordingly.

LIFEBUOY SOAP — the most famous carbolic soap, lasting until the early 1990s, when it was turned from pungent red to white toilet soap and without its carbolic smell. It was supplied to grocers in both cake form and long bars, the latter being cut by the grocer to the amount required by the customer. I have been told that in many households the servants were required to use it under their arms. The soap is still available in its red form from Indian shops. This is made in South Africa. See also bar soap.

LIGHTS — lungs.

LIGHTERMEN — the elite of the river who are in charge of Thames barges.

LIME — white calcium powder, sometimes in block form, for lime washing steps and walls etc.

LUMP SOAP — see block soap.

M

MACE — the lace-like coating of a nutmeg shell, used for flavouring soups and stews.

MANGLE — two wooden rollers adjusted and turned in an iron frame to extract water from sheets and towels, etc. after washing. Also used for pressing clothes.

MANTLE — small, soft pouch of material attached to a gas jet. It was lit with a match and flared up. Then the gas could be turned on, and when lit again the mantle glowed and gave out a most pleasant soft light.

MILK STOUT — popular between the wars with dockland women as a healthy drink. Lactose had been added to the beer. Much like the present Mackeson stout.

MOVIES — brown, shiny laxative tablets for adults and children.

MUSSEAU — slices of cold meat covered with vinaigrette.

MUSTARD PICKLES — like piccalilli but more mustardy.

MUTTON — a sheep more than one year old. It is lamb up to one year, hogget in its second, two-tooth in its third and four-tooth in its fourth. Hogget has both taste and tenderness. Older meat is good for boiling or very slow roasting.

N

NON-BREWED CONDIMENt — a popular "vinegar" for fish and chips, pies and mash etc., derived from North Sea oil. True vinegar is made from alcoholic malt or wine.

NUTMEG — obtained from the fruit of a tropical tree, consisting of an outer pulpy coat, with mace covering a hard shell containing the nutmeg. Grated to flavour puddings (such as rice pudding) and vegetables. Small pieces may be added to flavour brine. Said to have aphrodisiac properties.

O

OXO — stock cubes used much in Docklands in stews and gravies. A cup of Oxo and an asprin was often given to sickly children.

P

PEASE PUDDING — dried split peas that have been boiled in a bag to become soft yet solid.

PEARL BARLEY — a grain much used in docklands for soups and stews — especially Irish stew.

PENNY-DREADFUL — a cheap comic.

PICKLED OR SALT MEAT — see Brine.

PLUCK — the windpipe, lungs, hearts and liver, used for faggots.

PORTER — black, sweet ale, supposedly loved by porters.

POSH — a common Dockland word for richer or smarter people, derived from the demands of the wealthy travelling to India for a Port cabin Outward and a Starboard cabin Homeward, to be on the shady side of the ship.

POT HERBS — carrots, onions and turnips.

PUT-U-UP BED — a folding bed in the form of a settee, or couch, that was used in the parlour, or front room.

R

RED HERRINGS — salted and smoked herrings.

RENNET — a preparation from the stomachs of calves to curdle milk.

REXINE — an artificial leather, used to cover chairs.

ROCHELLE — a laxative.

ROLLMOPS — herrings rolled and pickled in spiced vinegar and onion.

S

SAGO — cereal made from the pith of the sago palm, used in dockland as a pudding, also for thickening.

SALT — sold from the shop or salt man's cart in blocks, to be grated or hacked off as desired.

SALT BEEF OR PORK — meat pickled in a brine mixture in a wooden tub or stoneware crock (or now plastic) to preserve it and add colour and taste (see Brine).

SALTPETRE — potassium nitrate, added to brine for preservation and colouring of meat. Chemists will sell it reluctantly because of its use in explosives.

SAVELOY — a bland, economical, orange-coloured sausage. A favourite in the East End, containing chicken, pork, rusk, etc. — once much tastier.

SCRUBBING SOAP — see bar soap.

SCULLERY — a small room for washing clothes, dishes and preparation of vegetables.

SEIDLITZ POWDERS — for biliousness (related to the bile, being sick or headache). They consisted of two powders, one folded in white paper and the other in blue. The powder from the white paper was slipped into a glass of water, followed by that from the blue. The latter made the water fizz. The medicine had to be drunk when the water was sparkling.

SEMOLINA — the hard, coarsely-ground grain of Italian durum wheat used for puddings and making pasta.

SHANDY — a mixture of beer and ginger beer or lemonade.

SHERBET — a flavoured powder that fizzed in the mouth. Used in many sweets.

SHRUB — a kind of rum punch made of fruit juices, spices, sugar and rum.

SNUFF — finely powdered tobacco, sniffed through the nose instead of in the form of pipe or cigarette. Wilson's, sold by the 1/4 oz., was popular. A brown handkerchief was sometimes used to hide the marks after a resultant sneeze.

SPRATS — a small herring-type fish, sometimes smoked.

STEAMED PUDDINGS — suet pastry in a bowl surrounding meat or sweet ingredients and steamed for a long time.

STEVEDORE — a man who loads or unloads ships in the hold.

SUET — chopped or minced beef fat.

SUNLIGHT SOAP — with Lifebuoy, a popular brand name soap. See bar soap.

SYRUP OF FIGS — a popular laxative liquid, sold in glass bottles.

T

TAPIOCA — cassava root, looking like small, white ball bearings.

TREACLE — the name generally used for golden syrup, though really black molasses.

TRIVET — a perforated metal disk on which to keep irons or pots hot in front of the kitchen range. Another kind is used beneath the basin when a pudding is being steamed.

U

UNLAID EGGS — eggs used, especially in coconut cake, taken unlaid from the hen when preparing the fowl for the table.

V

VINAIGRIER — a lidded earthenware container with a wooden tap, used for making vinegar from cider or wine with the help of a "mother of vinegar".

W

WALFISH — a snail.

WASHBOARD — A board with a corrugated wooden or metal surface with which to scrub clothes in a washtub.

WASHING SODA — a cleansing agent, now seldom used, but available as Soda Crystals.

WATERGLASS — sodium silicate in water for preserving eggs.

Whelks — or, as the French describe them, sea snails, or bulots. Bought cooked from the shrimp and winkle man and prised out of its heavy spiral shell with a fork, or already extracted from the shell. On the chewy side. Much loved by those in dockland.

WHITING — ground chalk.

Winkles — small gastropods in spiral shells. Sold cooked. Prised out with a pin. A favourite shellfish of dockland, eaten with bread and butter.

WRINGER — see mangle.

Z

ZINC BATH (also known as a bungalow bath) — before bathrooms, the zinc bath was taken from the wall and filled with hot water for bathing, and usually placed in front of the fire or stove. It, and a smaller, oval edition, was used for clothes washing with a washboard.

ITEMS OF ADDITIONAL INTEREST

A FEW CHILDREN'S GAMES

This is a selection of games, fondly remembered by those to whom I spoke: Football with almost anything round. Hopscotch, marked out on the pavement with chalk. Knuckle bones, provided by the butcher. "The bones", rattled to music. A clothes line used for skipping and swinging from a street light. Hoops. Tops. Grottoes. 2 pins a go. Marbles. Tom Tiddler's ground. Green man arise. Flickers. Cigarette cards, swapped and used for games.

SOME AVAILABLE SWEETS

These, too, are a selection remembered with pleasure by the older inhabitants to whom I spoke: Liquorice and sherbet fountains, or dips. Lemonade crystals, licked from the bag. Toffee, broken from the block with a hammer. Liquorice Allsorts. Acid drops. Bull's eyes. Fudge. Humbugs. Gobstoppers. Birds' eggs. Jelly beans. Little black jacks. Stickjaw toffee. Banana splits. Palm toffee. Jap nuggets and desserts. Raspberry tines. Milk bottles. Sugar mice. Plush nuggets. Liquorice pipes. Liquorice boot laces and rolled lengths with a sweet in the middle. Dr. Spanish. Tiger nuts. Plain or dark chocolate Walnut Whirls. Aniseed balls. Dolly mixture. Twists of barley sugar. Butterscotch. Treacle toffees. Fruit drops. Jelly babies. Packets of sweet cigarettes. Rock. Sherbet lemons. Peardrops. Cinnamon sticks. Brandy balls. Chocolate drops. Glacier Mints. Chocolate creams. Fry's Five Boys. Farthing golliwogs.

SOME BRANDS OF CIGARETTES

Of the many brands of cigarettes available in the inter- and post-war years, here are some: Woodbine. Nosegay. Weights. Craven "A". Turf. Pasha. Flag. Embassy. Kensitas. Park Drive. Senior Service. Capstan. Piccadilly. Tenners. Lucky Strike. Dominoes. Bandmaster. Lloyd's Scented. Abdullah. Airman. Darts. Crayol. Goldflake. Player's. Black Cat. Du Maurier. Balkan Sobranie was an upper market variety, as was Passing Clouds. Joystick was bought singly and cut to the sizes required.

SOME BRANDS OF TOBACCO

Old Holborn. Goldflake. St. Bruno. Skipper's Navy Cut. Golden Return. A.1. Capstan. St. Julien. Boars Head Shag. Three Nuns. Digger Shag. Golden Virginia. Bondman. Nosegay. Nut Brown.

INDEX

Aitchbone 13, 85

Allspice 12

Almonds 103

Anchovy 30, 33, 56, 57

Apple pie 113

Apple Tart, Mince Tart, Jam Tart and Turnovers 112

Apple tarts 12

Apples 106, 112

Arbroath smokies 14

Arrowroot biscuits 18

Artichoke soup 69

Asparagus 57, 68

Asparagus soup 76

Atora 72, 111

Avocado pear 27, 30, 54

Avocados and Fillings 30

Bacon 17, 30, 38, 91, 96, 97, 108

Bacon bones 12, 66, 67

Bacon fat 36

Bagels 13

Baked beans 108

Baked custard 48

Baking powder 111

Basic Meat Sauce 51

Basil 26, 56

Bath chaps 93

Batter 101, 107, 108

Batter pudding 12, 13

Bay leaf 12, 47, 66, 68, 82, 85, 92, 93, 94, 95, 102, 117

Beans 54, 92, 111

Beef 13, 38, 51, 55, 58, 79, 89, 90, 91, 118

Beef Stew 79

Beef suet 78

Belly of pork 96

Bicarbonate of soda 35, 67

Black Jack 12, 100

Black pepper 79

Black pudding 16

Black treacle 116

Blackberries 105, 106

Blancmange 117

Blancmange 13

Bloaters 9, 13

Boiled beef 36

Boiled mutton 36

Boiled pork 36

Boiled Salt Beef or Pork 85

Boiled Suet Pudding and Gravy 25

Bones 65, 66

Brain 15, 93, 94

Bran 120, 121

Brandy 102

Brawn 15, 17, 54, 93, 94

Bread 12
Bread and Butter Pudding 47
Bread and dripping 12
Bread flour 120
Bread Pudding 106
Bread pudding 11, 12
Bread Sauce 61
Breadcrumbs 43, 45, 61, 81, 93, 99, 111, 114, 120
Brisket 85
Broad beans 28, 34, 57
Broccoli 50
Broken biscuits 103
Brussels sprouts 39, 44, 50, 65
Brussels Sprouts Boiled in Butter, then Fried 44
Bubble and Squeak 39
Butter beans 12, 55

Cabbage 13, 39, 85, 96
Cabbage, Potatoes, Sausage, etc. 96
Cakes 12, 109
Calf's Foot and Cow Heel 95
Calf's foot 16
Calf's head 94, 95
Calvados 102
Candied peel 109, 121
Capers 33, 37, 50, 55, 56, 57, 59, 67, 86, 93, 94
Caper Sauce 50
Caraway seeds 12, 121
Carrots with Garlic, Butter and Parsley 28
Casseroles 70
Cauliflower 43, 50, 57

Cauliflower Cheese 42
Cauliflower with Garlic and Fried Breadcrumbs 43
Celery 13, 14, 16, 57, 66, 67, 92, 93, 94
Chaps 15, 93
Cheddar cheese 42, 75, 77, 98
Cheese 37, 49, 67, 73, 76, 83, 108, 121
Cheese Sauce 50
Cheese Straws 121
Chicken 15, 38, 50, 53, 55, 66, 68, 108
Chicken Soup 68
Chicken soup 76
Chicken wings 55
Chickpeas 31
Chicory 57
Chilli Con Carne 88
Chilli con carne 32, 52, 87, 122
Chilli Con Carne Powder 122
Chilli con carne powder 88
Chilli powder 122
Chilli sauce 30, 32, 33, 57
Chillies 32, 33, 55, 56, 57, 92
Chinese Curry Sauce 55
Chives 34, 37
Chocolate 62, 106
Chocolate chips 108
Chocolate sauce 62, 63
Chocolate sauce for Ice-Cream 63
Chocolate spread 62, 108
Cholent 13
Chops 38, 40
Cider 96, 102
Cinnamon 12
Classic Grilled Tomatoes 45

Cloves 12, 61, 66, 112
Cockles 14, 46
Cocoa powder 63, 106, 117
Coconut 109
Coconut Cake 109
Cod 14
Cod's roe 30
Coffee 17, 42
Coffee cake 103
Coffee essence (Camp Coffee) 103
Cold and Hot Dip Sauces 57
Cold meats 38, 40, 54
Conger eel 14, 16
Cooking apples 113
Cooking oil 38, 54
Coriander 28, 33, 38, 81
Coriander seeds 33, 37, 39
Corned beef 17, 38, 83
**Corned Beef Hash and Corned
    Beef Pie 83**
Corned beef hash 36
Corned beef pie 13
Cornflour 51, 52, 71, 89, 117
Cornish pasty 111
**Cottage and Shepherd's Pie with a
    Vegetarian Alternative 89**
Cottage pie 37, 52
Cow heel 92, 95, 102
Crabs 14
Cream 57, 60, 61, 62, 68, 70, 71, 105
Cream cheese 57
Cream of Tuna Fish Soup 67
Cream soup 76
Crisps 108
Cucumber 33, 54, 55, 57
Cumin 92, 122
Cumin seeds 37

Cumquats 33
Currants 10, 48, 62, 103, 106,
    109, 121
Curried Mince and Peas 91
Curried mince and peas 52
Curries 70
Curry 108
Curry powder 50, 55, 91
Curry Sauce 50
Custard 47
Custard 13, 47
Custard ice 11, 105
Custard powder 48
**Custards and Bread and Butter
    Pudding 47**

Dabs 14, 16
Digestive biscuits 62, 63, 103, 106
Dijon mustard 42, 49, 53, 67, 75,
    76, 77, 98, 121
Dill 12
Dried beans 12
Dried fruit 106
Dripping 118
Dripping 11, 12, 17, 38, 39, 40,
    41, 58, 59, 79, 89, 100, 101
Dripping pot 84
Duck 66, 118
Dumplings 12, 36, 72, 85, 110,
    111
**Dumplings for Soup (and stews)
    72**
Durum wheat 121

Ear 15, 93
Eel and pie 15, 17, 49, 82
Eel pies 14
Eels 14, 16, 82
Eels and Eel Pie 82
Egg and Tomato Pie 80
Egg mayonnaise 53
Egg yolks 47, 60, 61
Elastic band 114
English mustard 55

Faggot stew 99
Faggots 13, 20, 35, 38, 99
Faggots and Faggot Stew 99
Fennel 57
Feta cheese 27
Fish 50, 55, 68, 81, 108
Fish and chips 17
Fish Cakes 81
Fish cakes 36
Fish fingers 38, 40, 108
Fish paste 17
Fish paté 30
Fish pie 86
Fish roe 57
Five spices 55
Flapjacks 104
French beans 28, 57
Fried Peppers, and More 46
**Fried Potatoes and Onions, and
   Spanish Omelette 40**
Fruit 111
Fruit cake 13, 109
Fruit pies 15
Fruit pulp 105

Game 38
Game birds 96
Garlic 12, 28, 29, 31, 37, 43, 44,
   45, 46, 55, 56, 57, 66, 75, 79,
   92, 93, 98
Gelatine 82, 94
Gherkins 33, 55, 57, 59, 93
Giblets 68, 69
Ginger root 33, 46
Globe artichokes 57
Golden syrup 62, 104, 114, 116
Goose 118
Gooseberries 105, 106
Grapeseed oil 54
Grated Carrot Salad 27
Gravy 14, 25, 58, 60, 65, 90, 97,
   100, 101, 102
Gravy and Oxo Gravy 58
Gravy browning 55, 58, 59, 89,
   101, 102
Greaseproof paper 111, 114
Greek yoghurt 69
Green beans 34, 55
Green pea soup 76
Green peppercorns 33, 55, 95
Green salads 54
Greens 89, 97
Groundnut oil 26, 54

Haddock 13, 14, 16
Ham 17, 75
Hamburgers 16, 38, 40
Haricot beans 12, 55
Head meat 93
Hearts 13, 15, 99
Hedgehog Coffee Cake 103

Herbs 33, 34, 45, 55, 57, 59, 66, 72, 83, 90, 92, 93, 99
Herring 9, 14, 16
Hocks 96
Hogget 50, 84
Honey 108, 120
Horseradish 30, 57
Horseradish Sauce 60
Horseradish sauce 13, 37, 60
Hot Chocolate Sauce for Ice-Cream 63
Hummus 31
Hummus 30, 31, 57

Ice-cream 16, 62, 63, 105
Ice-Cream of Various Kinds 105
Ice-Cream Sauces 62
Icing sugar 55
Irish Stew 84

Jam 114, 115, 116, 117
Jam dumplings 12, 78
Jam Roly-Poly 114
Jam Tart 112
January King 96
Jellied eels 14
Jelly 13
Jerusalem artichokes 69
Junket 115
Junket 12, 13

Ketchup 30
Kidneys 15
Kippers 13

Lamb 13, 38, 58, 60, 84, 89, 90, 91, 99
Lamb's liver 97
Lamb Stew, Beef Stew, Sausage Stew, Rabbit Stew, and Sausage and Smoked Bacon Stew 90
Lard 118
Large Fruit Cake, Seed(y) Cake, Coconut Cake 109
Leek and Potato Soup 64
Leeks 50, 64, 65, 66, 67, 89
Lemon 27, 30, 31, 33, 82, 106, 108, 114
Lemon peel 29
Lentils 12
Lights 15
Liver 15, 97, 99
Liver and Bacon 97
Liver and bacon 13
Lungs 99

Macaroni 13, 56, 73, 77
Macaroni Cheese 77
Mace 12, 82
Making Bread 120
Making Chilli Con Carne Powder 122
Mange tout peas 57
Mango 106
Maple syrup 108
Marinated Olives 119
Marmalade 62, 114
Marzipan 121
Mash 36, 81, 94
Mash Variations 37
Mayonnaise 53

Mayonnaise 30, 57
Mayonnaise toast 53
Meat and gravy 111
Meat pie 13, 14
Meat Pudding (and Jam Dumplings) 78
Meat pudding 13, 78
Meat sauce 51, 52, 75, 88, 91
Medieval Beef Stew 79
Meringues 53
Mince and peas 108
Minced beef 14
Mincemeat 111, 112
Mince Tart 112
Mint 58, 59, 66, 67
Mint Sauce and Mint Gravy 60
Mixed fruit 106, 115
Mixed spice 12, 106
Monosodium glutamate 55
Mozzarella cheese 27
Muffins 26
Mung beans 55
Mushrooms 29
Mushrooms 12, 29, 34, 68
Musseau 54
Mussels, 14, 16, 56
Mustard 29, 32, 57, 94
Mustard pickles 11
Mutton 50, 58, 84, 89

Noxious substances/toxins 32, 57
Nutmeg 12, 48, 115, 116
Nuts 33, 62, 63, 121

Oatmeal 119
Oats 119
Olive oil 26, 29, 31, 37, 38, 40, 41, 45, 46, 51, 53, 54, 55, 75, 96, 119
Olives 29, 33, 37, 56, 119
Omelette 34, 40, 53
Omelettes 34
Orange 29, 106
Oregano 122
Ostend rabbit 90
Other Cream Soups 68
Oxo 58, 59, 65, 66, 78, 90, 97, 102
Oxo gravy 25
Ox-Tail 101
Ox-tail 13, 101, 102
Oysters 14

Pancakes 13, 38, 98, 107, 108
Paprika 29, 42, 51, 75, 76, 77, 86, 108, 122
Parmesan cheese 56, 74
Parsley 12, 26, 28, 29, 32, 33, 34, 38, 45, 68, 81, 82, 84, 87, 90, 91, 93, 99
Parsley sauce 14, 15, 49, 50, 82, 92, 95
Parsnips 50, 89
Pasta 13, 56. 67, 68, 73, 75, 76
Pastry 110, 111, 113, 121
Pea and Bacon Bone Soup 66
Pea and bacon bone soup 12
Peanut butter 31, 62
Pearl barley 12, 84, 90, 94
Peas 34, 37, 68, 78, 91, 97

Pease pudding 35
Pease pudding 12, 13, 35, 72, 85, 99
Pecorino cheese 56
Peel 106
Penne 77
Peppercorns 103
Peppers 29, 33, 46, 56, 57
Pesto 56
Pickles 93, 94
Pie and mash 14, 17
Pies 47, 110
Pig's Head 93
Pig's Trotters 92
Pig's trotters 13
Pigs 15
Pine nuts 33
Pitta bread 30
Plaice 14, 16
Plain and Delicious Mashed Potato 36
Poisonous chemicals 27
Polish boiling ring 96
Pop's Pasta 75
Pork 38, 99
Pork chops 39, 55
Porridge 119
Porridge oats 11, 104, 120
Pot herbs 90
Potato and Onions Baked in Milk 39
Potato Pancakes 38
Powdered garlic 122
Prawns 14, 30, 46
Pulses 28
Pumpkin Soup 70

Rabbit 13, 16, 90
Rabbit Stew 90
Radishes 57
Raisins 33, 62, 115
Rapeseed oil 54
Raspberries 105
Red beans 55
Red Beans and Hot Dressing 32
Red kidney beans 32, 87, 88
Rennet 115
Rice 12, 33, 54, 55, 68, 94
Rice pudding 12, 13, 33
Rice Pudding, Tapioca Pudding, Semolina and Sago 116
Rice Salad 33
Rigatoni 77
Roast beef 100
Roast Potatoes 41
Roast potatoes 118
Rollmops 14
Roly-poly 115
Runner beans 28
Rusk 99
Rustic Apple Pie 113
Rye flour 120, 121

Saffron 50
Sage 12, 45, 90, 99, 116
Sago 13, 95, 116
Salad cream 54
Salad oil 26
Salmon 81
Salmon and shrimp paste 11
Salmonella 53
Salt beef 12, 13, 16, 85

Salt pork 85
Sandwiches 36, 80, 94, 120
Sardines 33
Sausage 12, 13, 15, 17, 33, 40,
    91, 96, 101, 108
Sausage and Onion Pudding 114
**Sausage and Smoked Bacon Stew
    90**
Sausage meat 108
Sausage Stew 90
Saveloys 13, 35
Scallops 46
Scrag 84
Scrambled egg 53, 108
Seedy Cake 109
Semolina 13, 116
Sesame seeds 120, 121
Shallots 59
Sharp Gravy 59
Sharp gravy 93
Sheep 16
Sheep's fat 118
Sheep's head 16, 20, 94, 95
Sheep's Head and Calf's Head 94
Sheep's trotters 92
Shellfish 46
Shepherd's pie 13, 37, 52, 89
Shin of beef 79
Short Crust Pastry 110
Short crust pastry 82, 113
Shrimps 13, 14, 16, 46
Silverside 85
Smoked bacon 66, 67, 75
Smoked haddock 81
Snails 16
Soda bread 12, 120
Softened wheat 121

Some Sauces for Pasta 56
Sorrel 34
Soup 12, 16, 37, 50, 65, 75, 87,
    93, 96,
Soy beans 55
Soy sauce 46, 55
Soybean oil 26, 54
Spaghetti 51, 52, 65, 74, 75, 77
Spaghetti with Meat Sauce 73
Spanish omelette 40
Spices 65, 66, 72, 92, 93, 99
Spinach 34
Spleen 99
Split peas 12, 34, 66, 67
Split pea soup 13
Spotted dick 115
Spotted dog 17, 115
Sprats 14, 16
Spray 57
Spring onions 57
Steak and kidney 111
Steak and kidney Pudding 114
Steamed jam roll 17
Steamed Puddings – Steak and
    Kidney, Sausage and Onion,
    Vegetable, Treacle Pudding,
    Spotted Dog, Spotted Dick and
    Jam Roly-Poly 114
Steamed puddings 11, 15, 110,
    111
Stewed apple 47
Stewed fruit 47, 114
Stews 12, 13, 65, 90, 93
Stock 65
Stock cubes 118
Stock pot 11, 15
Stones 111

Strawberries 105
String 114
Suet 72
Suet Crust Pastry 111
Suet crust pastry 11, 72, 110, 111, 114
Suet puddings 25
Sultanas 33, 48, 62, 63, 106, 109, 115
Sunflower oil 26, 54
Swede 89
Sweetened condensed milk 105
Sweet corn soup 76
Sweet puddings 47
Syrup 100, 108, 111, 115

Taco chips 30
Tahini paste 31
Tail 15
Tapioca 13, 95
Tapioca pudding 12, 116
Tarragon 34, 69
Tarragon sauce 50
Tarragon vinegar 32
Tarts 47, 110
Tea 17
Thick Cheese Pancake 98
Thin Pancakes 107
Three Coloured Salad 27
Thyme 12, 66, 82, 90, 94, 95, 99, 102
Tinned fruit 47
Toad-in-the-Hole 101
Toad-in-the-hole 13

Tomato 26, 27, 33, 34, 45, 54, 56, 79, 80
Tomato ketchup 57, 58, 89
Tomato paste 30, 51, 92
Tomato Salad 26
Tomato sauce 73, 75
Tongue 15, 59, 93, 94
Treacle 11
Treacle Pudding 114
Treacle roll 17
Tripe 15, 20
Tripe and Onions 102
Trotters 6, 13, 15, 16, 66, 70, 92, 95, 96
Tuna and Beans 87
Tuna fish 67, 81, 86
Tuna Fish Pie 86
Turkey 61
Turmeric 37, 68, 69
Turnips 66, 67, 89, 94
Turnovers 112

Unlaid eggs 109

Vanilla 47, 117
Vanilla essence 47, 63
Vegetable Pudding 114
Vermicelli 13, 56, 73
Vinaigrette 54
Vinaigrette 27, 30, 32, 39, 54, 57, 87, 92, 95
Vinaigrier 54
Vinegar 14, 26, 29, 30, 33, 46, 51, 52, 54, 59, 60, 61, 82, 93, 94, 101, 102

Walnut oil 54
Watercress 13, 14, 16, 68, 71
Watercress Soup 71
Watercress soup 76
Wheat grains 120
Whelks 14, 16, 46
Whitebait 14
White cheese sauce 108
White Sauce 49
White sauce 42, 50, 67, 68, 71, 77, 80, 86, 95, 102
White Sauces for Vegetables – and much else 50

White wine 96
Whole wheat 121
Windpipe 99
Winkles 13, 14, 16
Worcestershire sauce 58, 89

Yeast 120
Yoghurt 57, 60, 61
Yorkshire Pudding (Batter Pudding) and Black Jack 100
Yorkshire pudding 12, 101

COOK'S NOTES

COOK'S NOTES

ABOUT THE AUTHOR

After a broken education in England and America, Jim Page-Roberts joined the RAF and became a pilot shortly before the end of WW2. Invalided out with TB, the disease returned when he was a medical student.

After art and theatre design schools he designed and painted scenery for the theatre and television.

Returning to fine art, he exhibited paintings in London and abroad. About to show his large sculptures in elm wood, a car accident forced him to change course.

He then wrote many articles for magazines and newspapers, mainly on the subjects of wine and gardening.

His first book, in 1982, was on vines. This was followed by four books on wine, a cookbook, and one on vines and wines.

Unable to find anyone who would risk publishing a book on the docks, where he had built a house and lived in the 1960s, he established The Mudlark Press in 1997. This is his fourth book under that imprint.